Francismdelvecchio.com

November 25, 2013

This is a continuation of my first book and set of letters to President Obama. It is a damn shame that we are losing are freedom and it is happening from within, and it is no surprise. We have been warned by many Americans in the media and politics that this was going to happen as we grew through the 60's, 70's, 80's, and 90's. Now we are in the next century and most of the younger generation are going to be blindsided even after we bailed out of trouble in 2008, but not completely. The Congress and the Obama Administration have set us on a collision course with history and the ruination of a great nation that fought for freedom, stands for freedom and is slowly losing freedom.

The government is destroying people's self-reliance, creating a bigger dependent class, fostering class and ethnic rivalry, and eliminating competition in the free market. There is little regard for the oath of office and the Constitution of the United States. Egotistical manipulation to gain power and votes for elections and media bias are the rule of the day. Lying and spying on the American people is SOP, standard operating procedure. The younger generation can't support the older generations as we have in the past. We have borrowed more money than we generate in our great economy and the leadership can't see the flaws and don't understand that sooner or later the money will run out.

We have lost our standing in education and foreign affairs. We are becoming an example of what will go wrong in a democracy and the three branches of government are steering us toward ambiguity and failure. The world sees clearly what we are and where we are headed and they are positioning themselves to take our place. Only many strong voices and extreme pressure when needed will keep America the greatest country in the world.

April 10, 2013

President Barack Obama

1600 Pennsylvania Avenue N.W.

Washington D.C. 20500

Dear President Obama,

You are taking a lot of heat over cutting something people don't have. I agree with the adjustment. People need to learn that they should not live their life depending on what the government will give them. The message you want to drive home is self-dependence and reliance. People don't want to take the bumpy road, they want the smooth highway through life and not pay for the maintenance. SO MANY PEOPLE LIVE THEIR LIVES ON THIS PREMISE, IF YOU DON'T HAVE IT YOU WON'T MISS IT. The cut you purpose is something they don't have and will not see for a year, how they can miss it. The irony of it all is, the tax money people have waiting for a refund doesn't bother them as much as something they don't have. Go figure.

Your fellow democrats turned on you quicker than you can drive a screw in wood with a power tool. This is why, when you were elected, you are supposed to be the President of the United States, not the democratic party. They are angry because you didn't keep your promises, well HELLO, what have they been doing after they took the oath of office. Why don' you all take the HYPOCRATIC OATH, the one where you will do no harm, standing by the Constitution isn't working.

Now that you have managed to piss off everyone, guess what, YOU ARE STARTING TO DO YOUR JOB. Now it's time to take it to the next level and get the GLOW.

April 11, 2013

President Barack Obama

1600 Pennsylvania Avenue N.W.

Washington D.C. 20500

Dear President Obama,

It is always the people that have the most that bitch the most. I can't see how the wealthy help create jobs when they hide their money to prevent paying taxes. I suppose you could say the place where they stash their money makes investments into the future. I don't think so. Small business drives this economy, big business drives the stock market.

You should start a panel of common sense business people to review the tax code and reform it. You will probably need the same thing done to Obamascare by medical professionals. If donating or contributing to a lobby is a business or personal tax deduction, you should eliminate it. The same with contributions, are they given from the heart or for the tax deduction. I know when I give it is for the good it will do, but I take the deduction because I am allowed to. Missing this deduction would not bother me.

There should be a reform committee that does nothing but look at laws and codes and reforms them toward logical and good business sense. The government has got to be sanitized, trimmed and made efficient. They keep passing new laws and we still can't provide enforcement for the current laws. Most laws just take up space in books and you probably feel the same way about my letters, but they will keep on coming.

You really need to address the education problem in this country and not with money. We do not have a standard grading system and averaging test scores to make people feel better lasts only a moment. Achievement last a life time, but being 26th in the world isn't what I call achievement.

April 12, 2013

President Barack Obama

1600 Pennsylvania Avenue N.W.

Washington D.C. 20500

Dear President Obama,

The budget heat is rising and the nincompoops are out running their mouth and as usual they don't know what they're talking about. Trumka turned on you like a rabbit dog. He cannot see past his own paycheck. Bernie must be trying out for the ringmaster at the circus. They all want to raise money to help stop the budget. What a joke, they are raising money so they can spend more money. They are a real bunch of deep thinkers.

Your tax records are out, who cares. I want to see the records of the people you hired and your democratic mouthpiece, David, you can add Rove to that list. They are two of the most despicable people on earth.

Why are you moving toward the center, maybe you should spell it out for Bernie, more democrats for the house, hello? Advise Bernie, 56% of the country is receiving some type of entitlements and ask him what will happen when the money runs out, and it will. They still haven't figured out that you can't cut what you don't have. The years we did not receive a rate hike didn't send the population over the edge. People adapt, they just don't like seeing the waste and fraud at the same time they are asked to sacrifice.

Jobs and a growing economy are the answer, but efficient and productive government is also the answer. Low unemployment and a growing economy, hide a multitude of sins and that is what you have now, the exposure of an inefficient government, on that not, you are truly part of the problem.

April 13, 2013

President Barack Obama

1600 Pennsylvania Avenue N.W.

Washington D.C. 20500

Dear President Obama,

The loan program for college students is a disaster waiting to happen. Even thinking about allowing congress to include student loans in bankruptcy is ridiculous. Most of the blame belongs on the greedy colleges and the sports programs they support. It seems everyone want to have equal rights in this country except when it comes to money.

Students with financial support should be treated the same as students without financial support. The student should be responsible for their education after high school. Plans for children's education should start when they are born and there should be a shared responsibility. The government sets itself up for failure when they make taxpayer's money available to the disadvantaged families. They have minimal interest in their children's education. This is a major concern for all parents.

I would support an education tax on everyone's paycheck. Along with this, colleges would have to accept every student that wants a college education. Students attending state and county colleges cannot be refused entry based on tests. They should all be graded on the same scale and the students that cannot perform should be counseled in other directions. However, their curriculum should be focused on their majors and liberal classes should be excluded.

Colleges should be paid like Medicare pays doctors. This is the amount you deserve for the results you produce. We have liberalized and dumb down our education system to the point where we have to give special consideration to foreign graduates to come to America and work. This is disgraceful. We need to take care of our own.

April 14, 2013

President Barack Obama

1600 Pennsylvania Avenue N.W.

Washington D.C. 20500

Dear President Obama,

The work the FDIC regulators are doing, figuring out a way to dissolve banks that fail, is counterproductive. Banks that get their money from the government, taxpayers and depositors should not be allowed to fail. The simple solution to all the risky loans, friends helping friends, and downright stupid investments is to put a cap on stock and bond holders' money. It isn't fair that the bond holders receive money from a failed bank and stock holders get nothing. The best resolution to poor investment is life time jail sentences for the executives of the bank and their insolvent subsidiaries. They get a go to jail directly card. A perfect example is Corzine, who didn't know where the money went. Why is he still walking the streets looking for the next person or company to screw?

The same should go for people that run city, county, state and the federal government. Making promises and using the taxpayer's money to get reelected is as bad as a bank that fails. People suffer for the rest of their lives because of these blunder, so why shouldn't the people that caused the problem suffer right along with them in jail. They should also be stripped of all their wealth.

Conversely, people that default on federal subsidized loans should be stripped of all government entitlements until the money is paid back. We are too quick to forgive loan repayment and too quick to lend money without measuring its intended progress. There are time when people need help and there are times when people help themselves to unjustifiable means. I will cover more about student loans in my next letter.

April 15, 2013

President Barack Obama

1600 Pennsylvania Avenue N.W.

Washington D.C. 20500

Dear President Obama,

This is another sad day in our history for the people of Boston and America. This tragedy should serve as a renewed warning to all how venerable we are at all events we congregate at. The efforts of law enforcement and homeland security have been exemplary but the hard fact is we will never be able to stop people that want to do harm to America. The odds are against us as long as they keep trying and they will. It is a fact of life that people dislike people that are more successful and have a better life style. That will never change and the politicians will never stop using as a tool to get elected.

Vigilance is our strongest weapon against these blatant activities. At these type of events, we are so focused on the event, which is normal that only well trained personnel will be able to recognize and stop this type of attack. Peace is our goal, but it goes against human competitive behavior to survive and succeed. Then there is the outright loony birds like the leader of North Korea and other nations. People are too busy staying alive to compete against their type of tyranny.

Ultimately, this can all be traced back to what people learn at home and in school. We can't keep sending a message that we have it difficult because other people have it better. Our message needs to be that opportunity is afforded to everyone and there are obstacles like greed, hatred, and the lust for power that stand in the way of living a normal life versus being number one. We are our own worst enemy.

God Bless the victims, their families, you and yours and America.

April 16, 2013

President Barack Obama

1600 Pennsylvania Avenue N.W.

Washington D.C. 20500

Dear President Obama,

It is evident that we need drones to servile major events in the future as well as cameras and more boots on the ground. This will go against people that are worried about their privacy, for them I say stay the hell home and hide in the closet. The privacy issue in today's internet world is a joke. The protection of people, especially children, and the capture of criminals is more important than privacy rights. Even though we are all created equal, we don't thing or act that way and measures must be taken that people will be aware of to protect them and our freedom.

I would not want to be in your shoes every time you have to attend services for lost Americans. The real irony is you are considered the most powerful man in the world and there isn't much you can do immediately except offer your condolences. That is a tough position to be in when the families will be looking to you for answers more than compassion.

The drones will help and the producers of these events should bare the expense. Events do help the economy, so it's time for them to help foot the bill. Safety and entertainment are the common goals for the future. Will providing more safety measures be the answer, not 100% of the time. We all know how difficult it is to catch a lone perpetrator, that's why people's camaraderie and vigilance along with drones, and boots on the ground are our best defense.

April 17, 2013

President Barack Obama

1600 Pennsylvania Avenue N.W.

Washington D.C. 20500

Dear President Obama,

The stupidity meter must be jumping off the scale in the senate chambers. Instead of you attending the aftermath of these tragic events, you should send the 54 jerks from the senate that voted against better gun control. Put tee shirts on them with a big "S" so they can't hide in the crowd. I hope none of them have to suffer a similar tragedy.

More reports are coming in every day that Obamascare is scaring the people. Unions are starting to back away, but it's too late. I believe Obamascare will be sanitized, repealed or become a crash site. It came out of the senate, which is not known for common sense legislation, and is being operated by the IRS, a lethal combination. You signed your name to the nemesis of your legacy. There will be a footnote in the history books, he should have read it before he signed it. The intent was admirable and right, but the road you sent it down was full of potholes and sink holes.

You are only as good as the people that surround you, but I think they are more concerned about themselves then they are about you. There is a glaring difference between good legislation that deals directly with a problem and broad legislation that creates more problems than its intended purpose, that's Obamascare. When the democrats lost the house, they should have put Obamascare in reverse and taken their losses. Now you have opened up Pandora's Box and it and those alien creatures, your supporters, are going to be the first to bite you in the butt. Good luck with that.

April 18, 2013

President Barack Obama

1600 Pennsylvania Avenue N.W.

Washington D.C. 20500

Dear President Obama,

I asked my cousin, Rick, and my brother in law, Sherman, what is their definition of a republican and a democrat. Logic applied in both answers and these gentlemen are true Americans. They concluded and I agree that republicans "THINK" and democrats "FEEL." This was an explanation given to Sherman long ago by a country doctor and fit their definitions precisely.

Thinking and feeling is great as long as they accomplish the same objective and I believe this can be done. The problem surfaces when both parties think of their own objectives first and the country's welfare last. This has become fuel for the media and talk shows. What complicates matters more is the lack of accurate information that would be beneficial to our legislators. Everyone has their own numbers and statistics and they don't match. Numbers can be manipulated to suit any legislation, but do you think after being 16 trillion in debt we need to be more accurate? We can put a rover on Mars but we can't operate an efficient government.

Imagine a government without debt and 46 cents of every dollar being used to help the needy and provide a better controlled education system for our citizens. Imagine all the children that attend school graduating with a skill or moving on to higher education. Imagine a society that thinks of themselves as Americans first and accept people for who they are and what they do.

I can't imagine this because the two parties that run this country can't stop dividing the classes and ethnic origins of the people. Being American is not enough.

April 19, 2013

President Barack Obama

1600 Pennsylvania Avenue N.W.

Washington D.C. 20500

Dear President Obama,

What is the point of passing legislation if you are not going to enforce it? Why was project 500,000, the relaxation of rules and the reduction of INS inspector's authority, to deal with immigrants coming into the country? This happened under the Clinton administration and was designed to bring in more votes for him. Why were the monetary requirements waived for citizenship at this time?

The answer is, IT'S ALL ABOUT WINNING ELECTIONS, and the result is that innocent people are being killed and injured. This is despicable. The two parties in this country should be ashamed of themselves, one for doing it and the other for allowing it. I believe the mascots are appropriate, a jackass and an elephant, one that is stupid and the other that doesn't forget and does nothing about it.

I don't expect you to do anything about the problem because you are part of it and march to the order of the party. It is never about America, it's all about the wrangling between a jackass and an elephant. Knowing this, you as a man I can understand your compassion for these victims, but you as a President, I can't condone your actions and that of your party.

We are all about bring criminals to justice except when they work for the government. There seems to be a cloak of protection that can't be penetrated. Some people are fooled by the rhetoric and the phony concern and the people that are not are branded by the political machines in this country. Needless loss of life generated by a ship of fools. Who are the biggest fools, the people or the politicians?

April 20, 2013

President Barack Obama

1600 Pennsylvania Avenue N.W.

Washington D.C. 20500

Dear President Obama,

What the hell is going on in your administration and the justice dummies? What would it have hurt if you read this terrorist his Miranda Rights. More is better and less got you on the front page again by this stupid move. I can't believe you are going to give this jackass special conditions. I hope he goes quietly and stops all the media hype and making the American justice system look dumber than they are. Who is doing the thinking down there, the mascot?

This is great, here we go again, and who knew what, when and what did they do about it? We don't know what happened in Bengasi, we don't know what happened with fast and furious and now this? What the hell do we know? Americans are dying and no one wants to speak up. I believe that is the case in this administration should be held accountable.

We need to stop immigration and get rid of all these persons of interest. Your administration has proven they can't handle the job, so shut the borders until we have control of the immigrants in this country. Keep the good and hardworking and get rid of the bad. Pass legislation to that affect. We pass it for everything else and don't enforce it, why not try something new. Yes, give the inspectors back their authority, stop accepting the Holiday Inn as an address, reinstate the monetary requirements, stop using immigration as a tool for elections and require proper ID for all voters. Get on with it.

April 21, 2013

President Barack Obama

1600 Pennsylvania Avenue N.W.

Washington D.C. 20500

Dear President Obama,

The Montana Indian water project that was stopped because the big chief stole millions of dollars is a clear example of why socialism doesn't work. We have been given to the Indians for over 300 years and they have made very little progress on their own. There are those that ambition hooked and they made a good life for themselves and moved off the reservation. There are those that are enjoying the settlement that cost taxpayers billions of dollars and there are those that will milk the system for all they can get as long as we give it to them. They are no different than other American who take advantage of entitlements.

There is no doubt, that when you pay into something you expect the entitlement to be there for you, but these program were not designed to live off of for the most of your lives. Liberalism has destroyed people's ambition and made them reliant upon government. Supporting people is not helping people. The best way to support people is making sure they get a good education and continue to be educated as the world changes. We have done a piss poor job in this area as well as business and industry. The schools and especially the colleges are more structured on political solutions rather than individual achievement. The people that do succeed are chastised because they are successful.

Politics in this country must change and I don't see that happening. The country is stuck in a rut and media has helped put us there. We need to get pass the imagery and focus on leadership and common sense solutions, not unfulfilled promises.

April 22, 2013

President Barack Obama

1600 Pennsylvania Avenue N.W.

Washington D.C. 20500

Dear President Obama,

Reality is starting to set in around the country regarding sequester cuts. People will have to learn to adjust to the changes and do what is necessary. The reality is the media is hyping all these changes because there isn't enough money, but we know that isn't the case. Poor management, waste and fraud are the real culprits in this budget mess as well as the donkey's and elephants in congress. Throwing money at every problem we face is not the answer.

Americans expect a certain level of services in our daily lives. Any change is climatic because we can't adjust quickly enough to the change. The facts are, what is not there will not be missed. We are a nation that went from being pioneers and change to a nation of convenience. It is not enough to get on an airplane, we have to bring our house with us and get annoyed when we are told no.

The attitude of the leaders regarding these cuts shows their inability to deal with the problem. Are they looking at the details or just trying to adjust the big picture. I believe they are following the road less traveled to make their trip easier. A perfect example of this is the pathetic vote on background checks by the senate. That vote should have been 100 yea, 0 nay, for passage.

I'll bet you didn't realize how much power the President doesn't have. Without support, you are just a good ole boy like the average American depending on others to do what is prudent and necessary. The profiteers of the media are loving your controversial successes and devastating failures. Rhetoric is only as good as the money supply.

April 23, 2013

President Barack Obama

1600 Pennsylvania Avenue N.W.

Washington D.C. 20500

Dear President Obama,

I am getting as bad as you. I didn't read the gun bill and that makes an ass out of me. Background checks online, how stupid. The people that need to know about the people buying guns are the police, not gun dealers. This would create more work for the police, but who knows their citizens better. I would have said NO to this bill based on the online background checks. I know most people put their business out there anyway, but this is as bad as the dopes who published names and addresses in the newspaper.

There isn't a damn thing you can do about the guns that are out there now, but there is something you can do about new purchases. My previous letters endorsed manufacture responsibility. Put chips in the weapons so we know where they are and hand recognition on the weapon so only the owner can use the weapon. Set up gun exchanges operated by the manufactures in all the states and have local police departments do the background checks. The manufactures and the purchasers should pick up the cost for this. This goes for foreign manufactures as well. The auto industry controls their cars, the phone industry controls their phones and some states have control over the liquor stores. The laws should be aimed at the manufactures. This was not a common sense law.

Legislation needs to be written so people can understand it. It should pass the laws for dummies test before it goes to congress. We have complicated the standard of living beyond comprehension. I believe that is the way you want it so you can remain in control. You talk the talk but never take the walk. Shame on all of us.

April 24, 2013

President Barack Obama

1600 Pennsylvania Avenue N.W.

Washington D.C. 20500

Dear President Obama,

I know how you can create jobs, build more prisons. We will need more prisons once Janet finally does her job and puts all the illegal aliens in jail until you decide what to do with them. I have another great idea, make them border patrol agents, who knows better than them how to sneak into the country. You can have Holiday Inn build more hotel since that is the main destination and place of residence for all legal immigrants coming into the country. Better yet, why don't we all move to another country and let them have America. This way there can be one political party, the democrats and they can wave donkey flags over the capitol.

I am joking, but the sad truth is the immigration policy in this country is a joke. This problem, like many others, isn't getting fixed because it's all about votes for the donkeys. One day the poor and middle class will wake up and find out that they are being used by the democratic machine. Their democratic policies keep them in the poor house and the propaganda machine keeps them misinformed. The truth is, when the money runs out so will the Democratic Party and its supporters will be left holding an empty bag of freebies and entitlements.

Start doing something right, enforce current immigration laws, protect the borders and create jobs by approving the pipeline with a law that all the products will be used for our domestic use and security. The price of gas, food and home energy will go down, poor people will have more money to spend and the demand for products will go up and more jobs will be created and you will have done something right for a change.

April 25, 2013

President Barack Obama

1600 Pennsylvania Avenue N.W.

Washington D.C. 20500

Dear President Obama,

It is obvious that the government can't perform at its best level when they are dealt with multiply tasks. This will be the case if the immigration bill passes. I would like to see a comprehensive bill, but I would rather see more results from the current laws first. The fact we can't control our own borders should indicate a clear path of failure for the rest of the bill. We must do one thing right then move on to the next. Multi-tasking is not a strong function of government. Government lacks discipline that makes our military successful.

Secure the borders and do it right, once done move to the next step of the bill and get rid of all the bad eggs. Sending them out with unsecured borders only means they will return. After this is functioning proficiently, move on to the path of citizenship. The point is build on your successes.

I can't believe after 300 years we still do not have an official language in America. This is the binding thread and a clear path for America. I don't care where people come from but I do care what they want to be when they are here. It is time America has its own culture. I don't care who eats spaghetti on Sunday, tacos on Monday, soul food on Wednesday or any other culture habits. There is only one flag to wave in this country. If people want to be recognized by their place of origin then send them back there and they can wave that flag all they want. While they are here enjoying the fruits of America, they must assimilate in our culture, learn English and be beholding to the country they live in. You are great at giving speeches, put more effort into leadership.

April 26, 2013

President Barack Obama

1600 Pennsylvania Avenue N.W.

Washington D.C. 20500

Dear President Obama,

The entire immigration issue smells rotten. What are people doing here that don't want to be here, that have been investigated by more than one federal agency for radical behavior, and are considered persons of interest? I don't get it.

The solutions are simple, the execution is simple, but the government doesn't believe in doing things simple and they can't do them if they are complicated, so why don't you start a new trend. Close the borders and secure them. Once accomplished, round up all persons of interest and criminal offenders here illegally. Sort them through all the agencies and determine who goes and who stays. The people that stay have to agree to a monitoring program, if not, ship them out with the people that go. After completion and the border is still closed, put the remaining hard working illegal's through a citizenship program. Once this is accomplished, open the borders to people that will assimilate to our society and follow the procedures for citizenship.

This is a radical solution, but not being as radical as the people that hate America is killing our children and families. I don't care if their feelings get hurt or their relatives don't like it, I'm only concerned about the hard working people in this country that want to contribute to America's continued freedom and progress. Sometimes you have to do things that will make you unpopular, tell the people the truth to the people, even if it's not what they want to hear, and demonstrate leadership. Taxing people, giving them freebies, and giving them feel good speeches that mean nothing is not leadership.

April 27, 2013

President Barack Obama

1600 Pennsylvania Avenue N.W.

Washington D.C. 20500

Dear President Obama,

College loans are forgiven for members of congress children? Did I hear this and read this correctly. Congress does not want to participate in the Obamascare program? Did I hear this right? I'm sure I did.

How can a man with a law degree who studied the constitution let congress get away with this? If I remember right, doesn't the constitution state that congress will make no law that gives them advantage over the people and conversely. Remember putting you hand on the bible and saying you will uphold the Constitution of the United States of America. I remember that, so why aren't you doing your job.

NO WONDER PEOPLE DON'T TRUST GOVERNMENT.

The Boston and Benghazi situations look bad, smell bad and make your administration look like the mascot of your party. TRANSPARENCY, transparency, OH WHERE ART THOU. How much of your staff spends time covering up and setting road blocks to the truth in your administration. Shucking and jiving is what the American people get, you may as well put music to it and sell it and use the profits to help pay off the deficit.

Do something about the loans for congress member's children. Are they still bouncing checks, you might want to look into that. Make a speech, your good at it, and let them know they aren't allowed to make laws that give them advantage over the people and tell them, NO, you are not getting an exemption from Obamascare.

April 28, 2013

President Barack Obama

1600 Pennsylvania Avenue N.W.

Washington D.C. 20500

Dear President Obama,

What a hypocrite you are. You talk about the congress coming up with a bill to support traffic controllers because they fly home on the weekend and how this will affect children and plan parenthood and now you will sign the bill. BAD MOVE.

GOOD MOVE. Sign the pipeline bill and make sure the oil is for domestic use, not export.

It will create jobs and that is more tax revenue.

The cost of gas, aviation fuel, and diesel fuel will go down.

The military will save money on fuel cost but they need to look harder at their budget.

People, especially the poor, will have more money in their pocket, not the gas tank.

The price to transport food and supplies should go down as well, more money in pocket.

You can stop out sourcing and create more jobs at home.

You can stop immigrating people in to work as out sourced wages.

You can stay in Washington, stop giving speeches, show leadership and save money.

The point is there is a lot you can do but you don't. I know your powers are limited, but I'm sure your handlers can manipulate a way to get this done. They did for Obamascare. Washington needs to get over the me first attitude and that starts with you. So how about it, you up to go for the three pointer or you going to keep sitting on the bench. The clock is ticking and there are no time outs left.

April 29, 2013

President Barack Obama

1600 Pennsylvania Avenue N.W.

Washington D.C. 20500

Dear President Obama,

Maybe you can enlighten me about our Constitution, I'm confused. I believe there are two documents that govern our behavior and help maintain our freedom, they are the Ten Commandments and the Constitution of the United States of America. They are the guiding instruments that made this country great. Now, we have something called the living constitution and congress talks about it often. So, what constitution did you swear to uphold?

Where did we go wrong? The congress makes laws that benefit them and that is against the constitution. They don't want to participate in Obamascare, they have forgiven their children's student loans, they are passing a measure to keep the flow at airports going so they can get home on time, not because it is the prudent thing to do for the safety of the passengers and crew, and their pension plan is an insult to every hard working American. There are representatives and senators that hardly show up for work and they spend money faster than the printers can make it. So, what are you doing about this, nothing?

Back to my original thought, you signed Obamascare that originated in the senate, what part of the Constitution were you following when you did this? It's ok for Washington to make the laws and break the laws and follow them when it suits them and you sign them. The pen is your weapon to secure justice for the American people. Obviously, you misread this when you studied the Constitution in school, shameful.

April 30, 2013

President Barack Obama

1600 Pennsylvania Avenue N.W.

Washington D.C. 20500

Dear President Obama,

You looked mighty uncomfortable when you were asked about Benghazi yesterday. Why does the media know more than you about what is going on? I really doubt it. It is time to fess up before this gets any worse. What happened there was tragic and we learned from it, but what will be more tragic is if you know more that you're telling and you get caught. You don't want to be another Nixon or Clinton for that matter. After all he did he survived and is loved. Do the right thing.

Obamascare is scaring the hell out of people because neither the processor nor the recipient know what is going on. Mega pages of rules and regulations and more to fix what they don't understand. You complicated a good idea, failed to read it and now you have a real a cluster puck. You should do the right thing and ask congress to repeal it and start over. Keep it simple, go for the coverage you want and let the insurance companies worry about it. You have to agree, the government is not the best processor for this program, waste and fraud will be jumping off the scale.

All the chicanery that goes on in Washington is planned to do one thing, keep as many votes for the party as possible. Americans, especially the uninformed and the I don't care, just don't understand, it's all about votes and who wins. Government never fixes problems, they react to them. God forbid either party does something good for the country without screwing it up and costing taxpayer's money. You have been treading water long enough, it's time to head for the beach and build your sand castle, and the new leaders won't care about you when your time is up. You don' want to be another Carter.

May 1, 2013

President Barack Obama

1600 Pennsylvania Avenue N.W.

Washington D.C. 20500

Dear President Obama,

Tell the president of Bolivia, he can go to hell. Stop accepting Bolivians in this country. We have spent enough money in that country. Their feelings are hurt and our wallets are hurt.

It is time to act and do something drastic. The borders must be shut to everyone until we can get control on the illegals and sort them out. The bad must go and the hardworking should stay. This is not hard to figure out. Stop worrying about votes and do what's right for the country. Man up.

Pass a simple law, any activist group, unions, religious groups and individuals that promote rallies and protest will be responsible for all government expenses, police support and property damage on an equal basis and all participants must sign a letter of intent. They should all understand they have a right to protest but at a cost if the protest becomes unmanageable and violent.

The hole you are digging on Benghazi and this mess in Boston is getting deeper. Come out of the closet and save your own butt. The Democratic Party is going to feed you to the fishes and they won't lose a heartbeat over it. You might be the president, but you have seen in the past they will turn on you in a heartbeat. You are only as good as the money flows.

May 2, 2013

President Barack Obama

1600 Pennsylvania Avenue N.W.

Washington D.C. 20500

Dear President Obama,

You're on the road again, amazing. I hope you don't give the treasury chest away. What was the point of this visit other than you want to be a nice guy? More wasted gas and money.

Your failure to close the borders is costing a lot of people their lives. What is so hard about doing this other than the democratic would lose many voters. There are people that don't like us and they are coming in everyday. You can solve this problem and won't. I suggest you don't attend any more funerals of this nature, as you are part of the cause and problem. If you stay home and take care of our problems first maybe we can move forward.

Benghazi and Boston, homeland security, who will pay the price for this mess. You can't figure out who is lying more the good guys or the bad guys. Congress wants a report, they are just as bad as you. They can move to close the borders so they are just as responsible as you are. Their immigration bill has a real good chance of passing now. Solve the problem step by step.

It's wake up time. With all the states passing passive drug laws, you think we may have a problem here. Where is the federal enforcement of the laws? I get it, it is okay to drink and drive drunk, so now you can puff and drive impaired. Let's legalize it so we can tax it. Good move. What a feckless, despicable bunch you all are in Washington.

May 3, 2013

President Barack Obama

1600 Pennsylvania Avenue N.W.

Washington D.C. 20500

Dear President Obama,

It is time for you to think of your legacy and do what is right for the country, instead of worrying about the Democratic Party. It is time to put the pen in the draw and support meaningful and simple legislation. Sign what makes sense, like the pipeline bill. I don't see too many environmentalists living in the woods and growing gardens. They probably wouldn't know what to do if you removed them from their cushy living conditions and took their cell phones away.

Your trip is producing mega results. The entire trip is like two people who have a disease and no one wants to talk about it. This trip is a real deal maker. Meanwhile you have the mental case in Bolivia who kicked us out after spending a couple of billion dollars there. You can see how much good we did in Egypt, they are asking the Russians for 30 billion dollars, better them then us. So much for democracy.

We have 435 congressional representatives, 100 senators, 9 judges, actually 8, one never sat on a bench unless it was in the park and there is you. At what point, and who will start putting America first. Let's start with a simple law and make English the official language. I just wonder how we can screw that up. No takers.

Maybe you are confused because of your golf game, you normally get 3, 4, or 5 shots to get it in the hole. Maybe that's why it takes more than a hole in one for the government to get it right. You all think you are on the back nine heading to the clubhouse for chit chat and drinks. If you could come up with good, simple and enforceable legislation on the golf course, I'm all for it.

Let me help you, drive the ball down the center of the fairway, best place to be. You are in good position and you have only pissed off a few roughens on the left and right. Take the next shot and stay away from the traps on the left and right. The competition can't wait till you screw up, so play it safe and leave yourself an easy chip shot. If you're lucky it will hit the pin and drop in the hole, if not, you need to leave yourself with a give me, even though they will push you to make the putt. Show them whose boss and drop it like a pro and don't ring the cup. After you played par for the course, don't forget to sign the card and smile. I hope this helps.

May 4, 2013

President Barack Obama

1600 Pennsylvania Avenue N.W.

Washington D.C. 20500

Dear President Obama,

It amazes me how the democrats were so quick and devious about getting Obamascare passed and now they are calling it a train wreck. The media reports on Obamascare every day, but I don't think they will ever keep up with all the new rules and regulations the IRS keeps adding to the bill. What nerd will be able to read this monstrosity and make common sense out of it? I think when all is said and done they should use it for wall paper in your presidential library.

The idea of insurance coverage for everyone is great, but that is not why the democrats pushed it. Votes, tell the poor and unfortunate you're going to give them something else and they will vote for you. The reality is that it will cost them in the long run just like all the other legislation that is and is not passed.

Economist do not understand pennies like poor and middle class people do. EVERY TAX INCREASE WILL RESULT IN COST INCREASES TO THE PEOPLE WHO LEAST CAN AFFORD IT. People and businesses are not going to let you take more money from them. They will figure a way to generate income to replace the increased taxes and that will trickle down to the poor and middle class, basic math 101.

How does this relate to medical insurance, simple, premiums are not going down? Supplemental insurance premiums are going up, drugs are going up, medical expenses are going up and there is no way to stop this train wreck or vicious tax cycle. Shifting the problem to the states is not the answer and neither is Obamascare.

May 5, 2013

President Barack Obama

1600 Pennsylvania Avenue N.W.

Washington D.C. 20500

Dear President Obama,

Selling the morning after pill, over the counter, to 15 year old children is a real testament to your morale values. Did you fall out of bed or get hit in the head with a golf ball when you came up with this gem. Are you putting a Surgeon General's warning on the box explaining the mental and physical side effects, or is take at your own risk good enough.

Why aren't you removing the judge that wants to make the pill available to all ages? Will this cover up a sex offenders D and A if he forces his victim to take the pill? Is the Democratic Party going to hand these out as commemorative souvenirs at rallies and conventions? I can see it now, "smoke the weed and take the pill."

Time for a reality check, have you been on the plane too long and suffer from lack of oxygen. The government insists on getting involved in people's personal problems and that is what this is all about. There are teenagers who don't know what a broom or mop is for and we give them the right to vote, smoke pot and pop pills to satisfy their hormonal needs. What are we doing to create their moral fiber? Oh, I know, we give them buttons that say, Just Say No.

The democrats and you have done more to destroy the moral fiber and self-reliance of the people in this country then any enemy holding a gun to their head. Is this what we are all about, pot, pills, and freebees? SHAMEFUL.

May 6, 2013

President Barack Obama

1600 Pennsylvania Avenue N.W.

Washington D.C. 20500

Dear President Obama,

    Writing to you is never a challenge, there is always something on the burner causing lots of heat and, naturally, you are in the middle of it. I warned you before, the people you associate with and help you run the government don't really care about you, it's all about the party. Case in point, Bill Ayers, big mouth, subversive, jackass, just like the democratic mascot. His justification of his pass behavior, supporting bombing and killing cops, bodes well for you. He should be your center piece as you walk in the door of your proposed library, terrorist personified. Brave enough to support killing Americans but not brave enough to fight for America. He and all his friends deserve a trip a one way trip to a deserted island.

    Benghazi, what made you think you could cover this up and move on. This will haunt you for the rest of your life. Tell the truth and tell the people you messed up and so did your administration. Fire a few people and blame Hillary, your good at pointing blame, and get it over with. It is a big mistake to think this will go away and Hillary will get elected in 2016. When the heat gets turned up they will toss you in the pan and never give it a second thought. Your usefulness will become useless at this point and over you go. The Democratic Party will declare innocents and that will leave you holding the bag.

    I can see it now, a big banner over your library, WHAT DOES IT MATTER, WELL IT DOES MATTER, and you will know how Nixon felt when the roof caved in on him. Tell the truth, some Americans will forgive you and some won't, but it might put an end to all of the speculation. The down side is you could get impeached.

May 7, 2013

President Barack Obama

1600 Pennsylvania Avenue N.W.

Washington D.C. 20500

Dear President Obama,

The media is doing a good job trying to discredit the people testifying about Benghazi. I haven't heard much from you either. Is it true they called the military rescue off and denied these people support? Did people suffer and die because of your feckless efforts and a bunch of girl boys in your administration and the military. I hope this is not the case for your sake. People can forgive almost anything, but cowardice is not on the list. Simply, doing anything would have been better than doing nothing and lying.

You need to talk to Rand Paul about his view on privacy. There is nothing private in the world today, especially the business world. If people are hiding money in other countries to evade taxes, their names should be listed daily in the newspapers with their affiliations. It doesn't make sense to support companies and people that won't pay their fair share and it doesn't make sense to tax them more because they make more. They are doing what comes natural, even for animals, protecting themselves. People are tired of giving to a government that wastes money and tolerates fraud at every level.

The NRA through its legislative support have covered up and hindered law enforcement long enough. It is time to take on the girl boys and put the gun manufactures in their place. They don't want government intervention, but they don't want to police their own industry. No one cares if you own a gun, but we do care what you are going to do with it. If all the money they spend on lobbying is used for industry control, this just might be a safer world to live in. Man up, Mr. President.

May 8, 2013

President Barack Obama

1600 Pennsylvania Avenue N.W.

Washington D.C. 20500

Dear President Obama,

Is there any democrat who thinks for themselves? The lame claim that republicans cut the budget and that is what caused the lack of security in Benghazi is a crock of crap. Hillary was in charge of the budget for the state department, not the republicans. All the money that is given to other countries couldn't be cut to secure our ambassadors. This is simple and plain poor management. The government waste and their attitude about the money tree is the lack of fiscal management by the people in charge is the blame for FOUR DEAD AMERICANS. Stating you take responsibility and demoting personnel who tell the truth is not the answer for the people in your administration who don't know what the hell their doing.

It doesn't take hours for planes to answer a threat over the Whitehouse, so why should it take hours to scramble jets in Italy. Moving the FEST team would have been something to show attention and concern for the matter. You chose to do nothing and the lame excuse Clapper gave regarding the talking points should have earned him the jackass award from the democratic party. The harsh reality is, democratic only feel for themselves and could care less about anyone else. Your answer to quell the masses is give them money and shut them up. Here is a tip, THE MONEY IS GOING TO RUN OUT ONE DAY.

The compensation legislation congress is proposing is a joke. Good employers take care of good employees. They don't need the federal government telling them how to run their business.

May 9, 2013

President Barack Obama

1600 Pennsylvania Avenue N.W.

Washington D.C. 20500

Dear President Obama,

Obamascare is too complicated for the government to handle. You are going to waste more time and money trying to convince people that Obamascare is what they need. The harsh reality is the 4 in 10 people that are not aware of Obamascare, probably don't listen to what you have to say on any subject. When this program starts taking more money from the poor and middle class, and it must because you can't cover all the young people without taking money from them, that mascot is going to kick you and the Democratic Party right in the ass. Young people want to keep their money to party, not pay health insurance premiums to supplement coverage for the old people.

The government has never been noted for its implementation of programs in an efficient and timely fashion. What you have here is a complicated mess and they keep writing new regulations to fix the problem and they are making it worse. This is going to flood the emergency rooms and cause long delays at the doctor's office. You went into battle without enough troop and supplies.

This will take more money out of people's pockets when they need it the most. Everything is going up and now this. The economy will suffer more from this move and that will decrease your tax revenue to the government. Harkin, a bright spot, you can go and borrow more money and put more people on the government dole. That will make the Democratic Party happy because that will give you more votes and destroy another segment of the population.

May 10, 2013

President Barack Obama

1600 Pennsylvania Avenue N.W.

Washington D.C. 20500

Dear President Obama,

If you see a stain on the windows in the Oval Office, it's probably from the blood of the four men killed in the Benghazi attack. I don't know what the secret briefing was all about, but what it should have been is a decision on who will tell the truth first. Don't forget to include you lied because you didn't want it to affect the election. If you had done anything to help these people you would have been a hero, now you look like the democratic mascot.

I would keep a close eye on Obamascare. When it starts to unravel, you will need to step in and make a common sense decision, something Washington is short on. You might have to make a deal and save part of it as well as part of your legacy. You can always blame the IRS for the mess it will create. Sometimes,

Mr. President, you have to think beyond yourself to see a clear picture of what you are doing to this country. If this is your true design along with the numskulls in the Democratic Party, you will be here for the chaos it will create but in the end we all leave this earth. So far I see a flimflam man, an orator personified quick to point the finger, mired in a maze of lies and misrepresentations, and a man void of leadership. You are powered by divisiveness and loyalty to the party, but never to the country that serves opportunity up on a silver platter. In the end, WHAT DOES IT MATTER, IT ALL MATTERS.

May 11, 2013

President Barack Obama

1600 Pennsylvania Avenue N.W.

Washington D.C. 20500

Dear President Obama,

I know you must be surprised by some of the amendments and regulations in the different legislation you sign as the people are. I can't believe you read all of the legislation and I'm sure your staff condenses it down to the main points. I have to question their competency when Obamascare is off to a rocky start and some of the democrats are calling it a train wreck. It does not help that you have the IRS administering and controlling the process. It looks like Obamascare fell short of the green and is at the bottom of the lake and you have no more balls to play. I hope this is not the case and you are able to tell the people I told you so. The only place they took a giant step like this was on the moon and they weren't sure if they were standing on solid ground either.

Student loans, how can college graduates afford to build a future when they owe more money than their parents mortgage. Making the money easier to get is salivating the greedy colleges. They are licking their chops on the taxpayer's dime. The greed in this country is motivated by the greed of the government and that is motivated by the waste and fraud they can't seem to control. The system is broke and needs to be fixed.

Let's see, we take money from the people and we give some back, that doesn't make sense. We give back more than we take in so we have to borrow the money we sent overseas, buying their products, so we can keep up with the expenditures. We bail out the banks and companies that managed their business into debt and we do it over and over. I believe a little leadership is called for here. What do you think?

May 12, 2013

President Barack Obama

1600 Pennsylvania Avenue N.W.

Washington D.C. 20500

Dear President Obama,

   The average salary of presidents for public colleges and universities is 414.000.00, according to the Department of Education. This represents one administrative person in a large body. The administrative costs for schools is way out of hand. The cost for college sports a travesty and I wonder how much the students have to pay to support these programs. Sports are important when everyone can participate, not a select few. Schools should be recognized for their academic achievements not their sports achievements.

   I could never understand why college educated people needed so much administrative direction to teach, pretty much, the same subjects repeatedly. I thought the idea of a college education was for higher learning and more progressive ideas being brought into the lower schools and the business world.

   You always tout taxing the rich, when it is your lack of attention to the basic problems for the poor and middle class that make these people rich. Just like gas and food prices have a greater impact on the poor and middle class when they go up a few cents, colleges raise their prices in major dollar increases. There is no equity in a system that has to make major LOAN programs available to students and then allows specific people forgiveness for these loans. This is as dumb as collecting taxes and sending money back at the end of the year.

   I suggest you visit the Department of Education and give them some much needed direction. While you are there you should advise them to stop giving money to students that come on visas for an education. Leaders care for their own, FIRST.

May 13, 2013

President Barack Obama

1600 Pennsylvania Avenue N.W.

Washington D.C. 20500

Dear President Obama,

The HITS just keep coming, you can't stay out of trouble. The yahoo's in your administration are competing for the most stupid. I don't think that career people will put themselves in harm's way, on their own, just so they can see you elected. The first thing you should have learned over four years ago is this is not about you, it's all about the jackass's that run the Democratic Party. You can only be protected until you can't ignore the obvious any longer, and you are at that point.

Loans to green energy that went belly up.

Fast and Furious

Benghazi, doing something was better than doing nothing.

IRS investigating conservative and Jewish groups

Associated Press phone record invasion.

The most devastating is the comment about the cute AG in California and 976 hours on the golf course. You are going to wind up like Tiger if you're not careful.

Listen, as a friend, I inform you the party will only protect you until damage control is viable, after that, they will serve you up on a silver platter. You are expendable. Ask yourself, do you think anyone thinks these people, that caused these problems, did it on their own. I don't think so. Who has the power to get this done using your name as pressure, Valarie, David, Soros, and the list goes on. I wonder, are you really the President or the flimflam man fronting for the party? Save yourself and your legacy.

May 14, 2013

President Barack Obama

1600 Pennsylvania Avenue N.W.

Washington D.C. 20500

Dear President Obama,

I have listened to some of your supports try to defend you and your recent revelations. Without a doubt, they give a new meaning to the word DUMB. I don't know how Carney will ever regain his credibility. It takes a special kind of person to take as many hits as he does. I can't believe you could subject a person to this brow beating, but then again, it's for the party and you are worried about the 2014 election. Don't worry, as long as you keep sending those checks, your safe and will get to dance another day.

How could you allow the Department of Education to send out regulations that strip people of their constitutional rights? Refusing accused student legal counsel, the right to present legal evidence and the right to face their accuser is direct violation of the Bill of Rights. I know you can't micro manage the government, but I suggest that all new regulations and legislation get reviewed by a nonpolitical panel and a concise report be read by you before you sign or approve it, or is this part of the parties plan to keep control over the masses.

Snooping into the AP news room, that is a real stroke of genius. You were looking for a leak in your administration regarding national security, I don't think so. There are many other ways to determine leaks in your administration and the first place to start is at the top of your party. Did you tell Harry to make that ridiculous statement regarding the IRS scandal or did that come from the party. DUMB, DUMB, DUMBER

Mr. President, I know you have some convoluted ideas and so do I, but mine don't affect the country like yours. I hope someday you will wake up and be a real President.

May 15, 2013

President Barack Obama

1600 Pennsylvania Avenue N.W.

Washington D.C. 20500

Dear President Obama,

Did someone wake up in Washington, they think you're a passive President? Dah, when you load your administration with feel good people and have czars that think they are driving in England, what does the congress expect. You have created more problems than you have solved. Very few people can manage from the golf course, unless you are building a golf course.

Your cronies have stripped students of their first amendment rights and you allow political indoctrination, but a person can't practice their religion. Students are graduating with a debt load that challenges ambition and success. Administrators and coaches are making huge salaries and the students are paying for it. Sports over education and politics over faith.

Gas prices, they are hurting the poor and middle class. The airlines has to collect 6 billion in baggage fees because of the cost of fuel. Make a deal, approve the pipeline with a guaranteed gas price. Build stability and insist that all oil be used domestically. Think out of the box, not out of your mind. A stable gas price of 2.50 or less is doable.

Border security, strip all benefits to illegal's other than emergency medical care. Put the proper steps in place for entry into the US, that are reasonable. Put Janet on the border standing guard for a week so she can give the border patrol what they need. Border security is a joke.

I hate to jump on gun control again. The solution is simple, put the onus on the manufactures where it belongs. Mr. President, glib, passive, and short on leadership.

May 16, 2013

President Barack Obama

1600 Pennsylvania Avenue N.W.

Washington D.C. 20500

Dear President Obama,

You need to push congress to pass a stupid law and it can be done because this seems to be their calling. The law should eliminate the phrase, I CAN'T RECALL, and be replaced with, I AM LYING NOW, but I don't want you to think I am. It is ridiculous how many people in government can't remember anything but they are making critical decisions. Maybe they should have to pass a recall test or lie detector test to determine the percentage of truth they recall. Sounds stupid but makes sense.

This is come to Jesus time. If you didn't initiate this by direct request or suggestion, it would behoove you to find out who the real president for the Democratic Party is, because it isn't you. This would lend credence to my previous letters that you are being used and sacrificed if necessary for the good of the party or the people you pissed off in the party. I suggest you save yourself or man up.

This was not done by rouge IRS agents who don't love America. Incentives were given along the way and I hope they were smart enough to get a get out of jail card if they got caught. I suggest you look deep into the congress and your party for the answer. Even though I don't think you're a great President, I believe you are a good person and I wouldn't want to see you reverse history and end up like Nixon.

An investigation outside of Washington is what is needed here. Follow the money Mr. President and you will always find political hack.

May 17, 2013

President Barack Obama

1600 Pennsylvania Avenue N.W.

Washington D.C. 20500

Dear President Obama,

Winning the election is becoming very costly to you. When you four years is over and your library is built, they will hang a sign on it, Most Notorious. It doesn't have to be that way but you don't seem to take advice from anyone except the party and I warned you what they will do when the heat gets turned up and it sure looks that way.

Obamascare, do you really know what the IRS is doing to this bill. Given their reputation lately, I suggest you do some micro managing before they take it in a nose dive. I agree with the concept that everyone should have insurance, but there seems to be better approach to the problem then what was written by congress. You cannot tax your way to helping people that won't help themselves. The food stamp and welfare program are perfect examples of that.

Food stamp cards should only be activate for products which they are intended. The DOA needs to put special codes on packages that will correlate with food stamp cards. Any items that are not coded should be rejected at the checkout. Cigarettes and liquor are items that should be rejected. I am sure if you asked Michelle for help in this endeavor, all products that would contribute to good health and nutrition would be on the list and detrimental products would be off the list.

Managing fraud and transparency are not your strong points, so I suggest you put people in place that will protect you and make changes for the good. You may continue to fool the illegal's, the immigrants and the uninformed but the core American's will push back when you push too hard. Losing the House should have taught you something.

May 18, 2013

President Barack Obama

1600 Pennsylvania Avenue N.W.

Washington D.C. 20500

Dear President Obama,

This is an amazing day, someone won a half of billion dollars and I didn't see your name near the headlines. This is like a hole in one.

Here is an idea to help you reduce the deficit, I have mentioned it before, have a national lottery. If the lottery reaches more than one winner, for example, 300 million dollar prize, have 300 hundred winners. Why would you want to buy this ticket, simple no taxes and it would spread the winnings all over the country? People will spend a million dollars faster than one person will spend a half billion. The government takes it share pays off the deficit and the people get their share and help the economy, which help the government. Win, win, and give it some thought. There needs to be at least one original winner before the split.

The food stamp program I suggested yesterday is doable and will save the government money. There should be a similar bill pay program for welfare and hiring people to regulate and process would be cheaper than the money lost due to fraud and never used for the intended purpose.

Mr. President, if you would approach situations with better common sense and follow thru, you could be one of the best President's this country ever had, but if you continue to rely on the democratic party and their slanted ideas, not that the republicans don't have their own, you would be like the flame on a diving jet heading for the promise land, I suggest you bail out before it's too late. You don't owe the democratic anything, but you do owe America EVERYTHING.

May 19, 2013

President Barack Obama

1600 Pennsylvania Avenue N.W.

Washington D.C. 20500

Dear President Obama,

There is talk of impeachment in the halls of the senate and congress and this is funny because if you looked long enough and deep enough you could impeach the entire government. You did what you thought you had to do to get reelected, it wasn't right, but it worked. Still, it will go down in the history books under the big S, but know how liberal teachers are these days it will not be emphasized.

You need to establish an emergency response team that will go in during and after a disaster and help with emergency repairs and rebuilding. FEMA is a bunch of paper pushers and they are needed also, but you need more hands and boots on the ground. Recruitment for this program should come from veterans leaving the military. It will help them get reestablished and learn a trade at the same time. The trades should cover all aspects of rebuilding a community and it should be done with local cooperation. Dishing out money all the time is not the answer.

One Sunday afternoon, you and Michelle should take a ride around Washington and promote a program to clean and repair that town. The nation's capital shouldn't look like the national dump.

I have a golf story for you. In my younger days, one day, I played golf with my father and my uncles. The first fairway ran alongside a rode lined with telephone poles and was straight and level. We had a bet going for the longest drive and they all down the middle. Me being the youngest and most pompous, thought I had this in the bag. My drive flew high and long before it sliced to the left and hit a telephone pole at a perfect angle. The ball rolled down the road toward the tee we were standing at and passed us before coming to a resting place. Naturally, I contended I had the longest drive, even if it wasn't in the right direction, but I was corrected and instructed to pay up. Needless to say my game never improved and there were few opportunities to play after that. I had no regrets but I still contend I had the longest drive. I wish I could have pursued the game, but family obligations came first and I wasn't a Bobby Jones.

Is there a point to this story, no, but regrets are a heavy load to carry. Sometimes you have to compromise even though you think your right.

May 20, 2013

President Barack Obama

1600 Pennsylvania Avenue N.W.

Washington D.C. 20500

Dear President Obama,

Oklahoma is a travesty. My last letter suggested an emergency response team for such disasters. These people will need protection and monetary help and I hope Oklahoma has the resources for that. I would tell you how to fund this program, but unless it was operated by a quasi-private organization, it would become a part of the mismanaged and fraudulent government.

The investigation into the IRS scandal is a joke. By the time the congress is done half your term will be done. Just a note, you need to find a better liar than Jay, he couldn't sell a used car. He would be better off stating we are not talking. Tell me Mr. President, who was the master genius who advised you to do the shuck and dive and burry the Benghazi and IRS scandals till after the election. I doubt if it would have made any difference, if you told the truth back then you would have been a hero.

The democrats and the republicans don't care about America, they care about their own party and who has control. Boehner has called for a vote 37 times to repeal Obamascare, what a waste of time and paper, but they have it on the record. The federal government is so big it is out of control and the one person that could do something is just as out of control. The founding fathers didn't see this coming. The level of stupidity, mismanagement and fraud in the government is unchecked and the information leaks are like Niagara Falls. You just don't know about them all.

The congress and senate is asking where was the President, but I say where the PRESIDENT is?

May 21, 2013

President Barack Obama

1600 Pennsylvania Avenue N.W.

Washington D.C. 20500

Dear President Obama,

I read that Loosy Lois Lerner would be put in charge of Obamascare, if this is correct, did you hit your head or something? The most private things, beside your gender, are your medical records and your bank account. It wouldn't take a genius to figure them out but the government doesn't need to help this along by putting Loosy in a sensitive position. This is like giving it to the dopes who published the names and addresses of gun owners in Connecticut. Then again, maybe you don't know about it. It is apparent you don't know a lot of what goes on in the Whitehouse.

The man taking the 5th in the IRS scandal should be locked up for protecting people who leaked classified information and his part in doing so. Just so you know, making the IRS scandal isn't making Benghazi go away. If that isn't resolved, Hillary can hang it up and start knitting baby shoes.

The more people learn about Obamascare, the worse it gets for this legislation. The union are starting to go against it now. Your friends at GM you loaned all the money to, we will never see again, will be the next group to throw you over board, but don't worry, I'll toss you a life preserver. I still think your intent was good but you relied on the democrats to write the bill and that was your mistake. There should have been a ton of input from the doctors, nurses, and insurance companies, not the drug lords. When you're ready to fix it give me a call.

The golf association is banning the long putter, it would be safe to support that move. Again, you need better support and information than you are getting, help yourself.

May 22, 2013

President Barack Obama

1600 Pennsylvania Avenue N.W.

Washington D.C. 20500

Dear President Obama,

You need to reassign Ms. Lerner or have her find an exceptional attorney. Why would you put this person in charge of Obamascare? The legislation is a mess to begin with and now you are going to put someone in charge that can't keep information confidential. Taking the Fifth Amendment is the say as saying I don't want to lie.

The environmentalist need to start helping the poor because they are a group that is keeping them that way. They obviously have money or they wouldn't have time to run around the country and demonstrate. Their message is clear, save the country for me and the hell with the little people. The charge that the oil is dirty is stupid, people are not taking a bath in it, and they are refining it for fuel and other purposes. Purposes that help them as well as every American.

Make a deal that will insure stable gas prices, limit exports, and monitor the pipeline for failures. If the oil is dirty, back the technology that will make it clean at point of origin and send it down the line. Think beyond the election of 2014 for the dumb ass party you represent.

Cruz is right, neither party can be trusted, because they each have their own agenda, and it isn't helping America. How can 535 independent thinkers come up with any solutions that are right for the country, when they all have their own agendas and think they should come first? Cruz is right and you are wrong.

The purpose of the immigration bill is not to legalize people so they can collect welfare and other government handouts. They're friends today, your downfall tomorrow.

May 23, 2013

President Barack Obama

1600 Pennsylvania Avenue N.W.

Washington D.C. 20500

Dear President Obama,

Your administration doesn't want the press to report your so called secrets, the old guard in the congress doesn't want the tea boys to hold up legislation, the IRS doesn't want to testify, the Whitehouse claims you didn't know anything, they want to raise the debt ceiling again, Obamascare has the unions angry, and on and on and on. On top of this you have prosecuted more leakers than all previous administrations combined. DO YOU GET THE FEELING THAT YOU ARE NOT WELL LIKED AND THE WHISTLE BLOWERS ARE WORKING OVERTIME, IF NT, WAKE UP.

It is dumb to mess with the first amendment and make the press the victim. What you are doing to Fox, the AP and others is downright stupid, and you don't know about it. Maybe they can't find you because you are on the golf course or vacation. Sooner or later this is all going to bite you in the butt and your friends in the Democratic Party are going to toss you overboard like chum.

I know, you think you are doing a great job and this is a nut writing these letters, I don't think so. Some thing you do good but most things you mess up. If you tell the truth without looking at the prompter and explain your views, any blind man can see, and be honest, maybe you can clear the way to leading the country out of the mess you have created, not George Bush's mess, your mess.

Understand this, the pen and peoples' thirst for the, I got you and will get you, have brought down greater people than you. The Teflon Don got ratted out and all the little rats nibbling at you will turn into Willard. The Fifth Amendment will not save you.

May 24, 2013

President Barack Obama

1600 Pennsylvania Avenue N.W.

Washington D.C. 20500

Dear President Obama,

Brad Woodhouse, the head of the DNC, has got to be dumber than a stick. How can you deny documents signed by Lerner and Holder and now Sibelius strong arming private companies? You can't make this up. You can't claim you don't know or you will go down as one of the most misinformed, a polite way of saying dumb, president ever.

Holder lies to congress and Lerner takes the fifth and sooner or later you will be the target of their incompetence. Your people are walking all over congress and I don't think they like it. Obviously they will try and get away with as much as possible. Your big mistake is back stabbing the press, conservative and liberal or progressive, the new word for liberal. Dumb, dumb, dumb.

Why would the media publish and broadcast falsified documents. What would they have to gain by tarnishing their image? The truth of the matter is you think you can get away with anything but there are too many people in the right places that don't like you and are singing like birds. You are way pass the I don't know stage and the final straw is Obamascare. That doesn't have bumps in the rode, it has sinkholes.

Even in Clinton's worst years and scandals, he managed to work with congress and get things done. He had a better economy than you so it was easier and you got stuck with part of his mess. I never hear you complaining about him. Mr. President, you need to get your act together. Stop borrowing money, revise Obamascare, sign the pipeline bill, get rid of the dummies in office, and tell the truth, it will actually create less problems for you.

May 25, 2013

President Barack Obama

1600 Pennsylvania Avenue N.W.

Washington D.C. 20500

Dear President Obama,

Let's put the scandals aside and talk about immigration. I am in favor of stopping all Islamic people from entering the US. Obviously, they don't like American and just as obvious, you can't see that. It isn't right to punish the majority for a few, but this is not the case. The few have control over the majority and they are set on a path of destruction. It is like fighting in Viet Nam all over again, you can't tell the good from the bad. The difference is the fight is on our soil.

The Islamic leaders over here are not stepping up to the plate and deterring this behavior from its members. I don't see them killing each other over here, just Americans. I'm sure your Mother told you to stay away from people that don't like you, so why are we allowing them in the country. Look at what they are doing in Sweden, the crown of liberalism. They don't want to change and assimilate into the society, so let them stay home. They come over for the benefits like all other immigrants, but others take advantage of the help and progress off the support roles. There should be a time limit on all support for immigrants.

It is time to tell the Islamic leadership to make a concerted effort and provide information that will help stop the radicals from coming here and get rid of the ones that are here already. The only war on terrorism that is over is the cooperation and support we never get from the Islamic community. The time has come for them to be excluded from the opportunities America has to offer until they can demonstrate peace throughout the world. It is time for you to forget your roots and do what is right for America.

May 26, 2013

President Barack Obama

1600 Pennsylvania Avenue N.W.

Washington D.C. 20500

Dear President Obama,

Politics today has three agendas, democrats, republicans and personal egos. America is the talking point but not the point. I can imagine when issues are discussed, the question always comes up, how will that affect the party and the elections. There is one representative for every 650,000 people, so why do they represent so few when they cast their votes. Lobbyist and money talk in Washington, not the people. Elections are the driver for legislation, not the people. Benefits and ego building are the motivation and not the people. I'll give you some good examples.

Immigration, how many laws do we need to enforce a law that states it is illegal to cross the border without proper documentation. One law, one consequence.

Budget, how many laws and chances do we need to enforce the law that the budget be done on time, and why NO CONSEQUENCES?

Why isn't there a law that gives the people the right to discipline the senators and congressmen that break the law? Who granted them the right of internal investigation and punishment, themselves, how productive and progressive?

The solutions are simple and the job justification for congress is complicated. Prim, proper and all full of crap. The gang of eight, don't alter our bill after reviewing 300 amendments and rubbing each other's back to keep their little piece legislation. The process is flawed. The tax code is flawed. The government performance is flawed. The election process is flawed, and most of all the influence of the few over the many is flawed. So what do we do about it, nothing, as usual? It's about the parties.

May 27, 2013

President Barack Obama

1600 Pennsylvania Avenue N.W.

Washington D.C. 20500

Dear President Obama,

It doesn't take a genius or newspaper articles to figure out that making new laws because government fails to enforce the old laws is just job justification and prominence in the media. You would know that better than anyone since you are always the talking point. You still have time to fix Obamascare before it shrinks the democratic ranks in the house. Your legacy could include imploding the democratic ranks in the house and losing the senate also. Remember, it's all about the party and not about you.

The war on terror is over, I doubt it. The hate for America is inbreed in them and they are for world dominance. They can't accept that there are other religious beliefs. The war on terror will never be over, but you need to do a better job of managing it before it causes another tragedy. Most people never understand this until it hits close to home and you are one of these people. The problem is, your plan isn't working. I can't see how sending troops all over the world to fight is keeping peace and protecting America. We need a better plan than that. People need to fight their own battles, we can't do it for everyone.

What would democrats do without New York, Illinois, and California, probably lose every election? Which states beside New Jersey have the most financial problems? Is there a clue in here somewhere? Sweden is learning the hard way about liberal payouts and so will we eventually. We are closer than you think. People and business will run fast when the fed starts tightening up the money and the market tanks again. The saving grace is companies are learning they can get just as much production with less people. The government needs to follow that leader. God save America, the leadership can't or won't.

May 28, 2013

President Barack Obama

1600 Pennsylvania Avenue N.W.

Washington D.C. 20500

Dear President Obama,

You were in Jersey and you didn't stop by, I'm disappointed. Lately, no news is good news for you and today is no different. More snitches are coming out and exposing your agenda and your people. There is so much lying and deceit, a special word will have to be added to the dictionary to describe it. Sibelius is your latest cross to bear, 54 million dollar slush fund to hire NAVIGATORS to steer the poor and disadvantaged to the Obamascare. Nice move, if it works. Didn't she get into trouble for snooping into people's business in 2008?

Now we have the immigration bill that gives a business a 3,000.00 incentive to hire a legalized immigrant over a citizen because they are not covered by Obamascare for ten years. This presents a constitutional question because you can't separate people's rights, therefore they will be entitled to Obamascare and all rights of a citizen. We both know it won't be long before this hit's the Supreme Court and helps enlarge the democratic voting base.

All this lying and deceit is about getting information and building a larger base for the Democratic Party. This is not about America and freedom, it stinks of communism and dictatorial powers. When the next snitch comes out and informs the people that the DNC is holding all the information and generating a watch list for loyal Americans, the lid will blow off and you will all be heading for the caged hotel. This sounds farfetched but I don't think so.

Why social medicine, why an immigration bill full of constitutional challenges, why information gathering by the Sibelius navigators, why snooping into the press, why the IRS inquiries, and most of all, why aren't you doing anything about it?

May 29, 2013

President Barack Obama

1600 Pennsylvania Avenue N.W.

Washington D.C. 20500

Dear President Obama,

They estimate that about 20% of doctors will refuse to take Medicare and insurance because of the short fees and the administration cost to collect the fees. The IRS has added over 500 new codes and this will make the problem worse. You don't have enough doctors and nurses to provide service for Obamascare once it starts in 2014 and you will have less when the doctors start dropping the plan. This was good planning by the democrats who wrote Obamascare. You need to repeal it and start over again with people that have a vested interest in the patients, not the democratic.

Holder wants to have an off the record meeting with the executives of the press. This is dumb on dumb. Isn't he in enough trouble for illegal investigations? I wonder how many judges turned him down before he found one who would sign off on dumb move. He wants an off the record meeting with people he is investigating, why bother?

Try this on for size, if Holder lies to congress then he must be lying to you. The other case might be, maybe you told him to lie to congress and you are the guiding light behind all the scandals. If this is the case how fast do you think they will crack if they have to face jail time, and I thought you weren't a gambler?

Who is approving all the rules and regulations the IRS is making for Obamascare? You think you will take the house back for 2014, I don't think so. Your only hope is that the uninformed stay uninformed and the entitlement programs keep paying the money. Blaming the republicans for doing nothing in congress just shows your lack of leadership. I stated before, as bad as Clinton was, he still was able to work with congress and get thing done. You need to get rid of Sibelius, Holder, and all you Czars who do nothing.

May 30, 2013

President Barack Obama

1600 Pennsylvania Avenue N.W.

Washington D.C. 20500

Dear President Obama,

I believe that every mother and father have told their children that lying will always catch up to you and get you in more trouble. Politicians, in general, call it twisting the truth or hiding the facts. I am starting to believe you all attend a secret seminar that teaches you how to disguise lying while you are speaking to people. In your case, Mr. President, I believe you genuinely believe yourself, so you can't tell the difference and you won't believe or accept the truth.

Look at Obamascare, who states the rates are going up and who states the rates are going down, WHAT DOES IT MATTER NOW, the truth will soon come out and you will be a hero or a liar. The way things are going, probably the latter, but I am sure you will find someone to blame because you can do no wrong. Accountants are great at manipulating numbers and politicians are masters at manipulating the truth, and you are the GRAND PUPA. Just remember, mothers and fathers are always right when it comes to lying.

Anyone with a half a brain or one hand tied behind their back knows rates will go up. Why? You have limited the menu and therefore limited the choice. The basic plan will eliminate lesser plans that cost less money forcing people to buy the basic plan. Their rate will go up just on that fact alone. Now when you turn 40, you will have to go to a different plan which is more expensive than the basic plan, no matter how healthy you are. You have limited the menu and the choice, sounds socialistic to me. What do you think?

It is fair to warn you, I have put all my letters in a book that will be published. I will continue my quest of true speech and good advice and send you an autographed copy.

May 31, 2013

President Barack Obama

1600 Pennsylvania Avenue N.W.

Washington D.C. 20500

Dear President Obama,

Regarding the scandals, what you knew versus what you didn't know, demonstrates an administration that surpasses the President. If you didn't know, then who on your staff gave the IRS the direction to challenge the conservative organization and where did the information go. It is poor management when you don't know what goes on in your own house. According to the IRS there were 88 people involved. One person might do it on their own, not 88. Someone is going to jail.

Do yourself a favor and fire Holder, Sibelius, and the rats on your staff. You need to personally get in Lerner's face and find out who started this mess and follow the line to the end. The only reason you're not doing this is you might be the end.

Obamascare for small business is being delayed for a year because it is too complicated to understand and put into force, how dumb. People with preexisting conditions are being denied insurance because money is running short, how dumb is this. I stated before and I will say it again, start over and do it right. People will think better of you, your party won't like it but the people will. Who do you owe your soul too?

Student loans should be zero interest with mandatory pay back, this includes everyone, especially congressmen's children. Why are we giving money to foreign students and why does the immigration bill have special clauses for talented foreign students and graduates. If you are going to keep the department of education, then put someone there that puts Americans first and knows what the hell their doing.

You need to make up your mind, who is running the Whitehouse, you or Alex or Valarie or the Democratic Party. You took an oath to uphold the Constitution, not the democrats.

June 1, 2013

President Barack Obama

1600 Pennsylvania Ave N.W.

Washington D.C. 20500

Dear President Obama,

I have noticed that you do not take advice very well, no revelation on my part, however people still can't figure you out. You are the front man for a bunch of democrats who want to seize power and keep it. You are perfect for the job, short on talent and long on rhetoric, the flimflam man. Your ideas are good but your follow up and implementation are terrible, and yes, you are responsible for that also, the perfect dupe.

I sent you an idea for the food stamp program so that people could only purchase the recommended food and supplies they need. You could have a special bar code on the packages that would allow them to pay with food stamps and you could continue to use the ATM card. No, you would rather see the fraud and waste mount up instead of making sure children and needy people get the food and supplies they need, so be it. Forty seven percent of the country on entitlement, great accomplishment.

You still haven't fired Holder, Sibelius, David and Valarie, what are you waiting for? They have led you down the primrose path and you're sucking it up. You do that in sports, not politics. Man up or are the only balls you have are in your golf bag.

Congress has accomplished nothing, just like you. Why don't you send them a bill making English the written and spoken language of the United States? That shouldn't be too hard to pass, maybe. Better yet, send them home on unpaid administrative leave, for lack of performance. Why do we need more laws if we can't enforce the ones we have?

Just so you know, it is time to bring the troops home. You can't teach democracy in religious based countries. Sooner or later the people will take over, but not when religion is the driving force. There is too much killing in the name of GOD, not winnable.

June 2, 2013

President Barack Obama

1600 Pennsylvania Avenue N.W.

Washington D.C. 20500

Dear President Obama,

The leaders of the Islamic religion, want special protection that will usurp the freedom of speech. What right do they have to anything special to protect their religion over all the other religions in the country? We allow them in the country, they do not assimilate to our society, they have no respect for woman's rights, they believe in world domination, they are totally against democracy and now they want special treatment so their religion can't be criticized. If they don't like the way we do things here, what was their motivation to come here other than to get money and start trouble. Everywhere they go they start trouble, Europe and Sweden for example. What is worst you pander to them. Your behavior as the President is disgusting.

Obamascare, what a mess, the people with preexisting conditions are being refused health care, the rates are going up on the younger generation, the law requires a special change when you turn 40, there are too many different plans, and you signed a law that you know nothing about. DUMB. If you are an example of the quality coming out of Harvard University, they should close their doors. It is well known, by intelligent people, that Harvard has a political agenda that is superior to their educational curriculum, and you are a perfect example of it.

REPEAL OBAMASCARE, FIX IT, TOTAL HEALTH COVERAGE IS A GOOD THING IF YOU DO IT RIGHT.

STOP OUTSOURCING

SIGN A PROFITABLE PIPELINE BILL FOR AMERICA

BRING HOME THE TROOPS

FIRE HOLDER, SIBELIUS, LERNER, AXELROD, JARROD, and the CZARS.

June 3, 2013

President Barack Obama

1600 Pennsylvania Avenue N.W.

Washington D.C. 20500

Dear President Obama,

I believe Issa is right, Carney is a paid liar and that is the nature of his job. He is supposed to spin the truth and dodge bullets to make you and the donkeys look good. The problem is, he doesn't have much ambiguity to work with. Lying doesn't work and it is going to cost you dearly. It is bad enough you pried into people's lives, but you also had other agencies investigate and harass these people. DUMB. Now you want Carney to go tell the press it isn't so, we didn't know. Then you compound the problem by having other donkeys complain that the elephants are picking on you. What do you expect, roses!

You will never have a peaceful moment as long as you continue to push Obamascare. I get tire of hearing about its failures and lack of implementation. All the studies are crunching the numbers to make you look good or bad and predicting more or less deaths because of Obamascare. How the hell do they know who is going to live and die. It shouldn't be part of the equation. Now we have more doctors jumping ship, so let's see, less doctors, more patients, equal longer delays for medical attention and overloaded emergency rooms, that sounds like it equals more deaths and I didn't need numbers.

It is time to bring home the troops and stop wasting money. It is time to set up a disaster group that can respond and help victims when natural and accidental disasters happen. This group will help with the physical and medical work, not pushing paper. You can recruit them from the veterans that leave the military. Do something positive for a change. You can also hire them to help enforce the laws that congress passed, instead of having them make new laws to cover the old laws. What the country really needs is a smaller more efficient congress as well as a federal government. Great idea, right.

June 4, 2013

President Barack Obama

1600 Pennsylvania Avenue N.W.

Washington D.C. 20500

Dear President Obama,

      I watched some of the hearings on the IRS scandal and listened to McDermott chastise these organizations for asking for nonprofit status. He is a member if the Democratic Party which is nonprofit, so where does he get the nerve to criticize other organizations for asking for the same privilege. This is what is wrong with government, looking out for party interest over American interest.

      Democratic senators sent letters to the IRS to investigate these select organizations, The IRS followed this direction, there are secret email accounts being used by the democratic party, you created the housing crisis and bank failures, you supported the unions in the financial crisis, you created this monstrosity called Obamascare that continues to invade people's rights and have put political interest over the safety of America. This doesn't sound like a political party as much as it resembles a terrorist organization. Your total lack of respect for the Constitution is obvious and your referral to it as an outdated document is subversive, while, at the same time, you operate under its protection.

      I never hear you criticize your party for the under handed politics and stupid decisions they make on your behalf. You are a party of nincompoops that prey on the poor and the misinformed by rewarding them for their support with entitlement programs that operate mismanaged and fraudulent. You fill your ranks with incompetence and degenerates that have tried to destroy America. The worst part about asking you to resign is that your replacement is worse than you and that doesn't say much for you. Your party and your performance have reached new low in American politics. You should be ashamed of yourself for turn your back on an America that has provide for you.

June 5, 2013

President Barack Obama

1600 Pennsylvania Avenue N.W.

Washington D.C. 20500

Dear President Obama,

You made the press mad and now they are coming at you from all angles. The economy isn't recovering, the IRS scandal isn't going away, Holder makes blunder after blunder, Sebelius is doing illegal fund raising, the donkeys are turning on you and your administration is as transparent as looking thru the black hole. Good job.

You need to get your butt over to the different agencies and show your face and tell the department heads you will not tolerate their behavior and their taking the fifth when asked to testify. I know it would be difficult for you to do that when all the testimony might lead back to the Whitehouse, but do a Clinton, say you're sorry and deny it at the same time and hope you don't lose your lawyers license. You may need it as much as Nixon did.

Why do your secretaries and czars need secret emails? Are they planning a war on the American society, you bet they are or they would not have to do it in secret? The lowest form of people on this earth is when you use other people to save your own hide. Just like I stated before, you threw Rice under the bus and the truth comes out. Lying is not the way to go, plead lack of experience on the job. You need to corral all the donkeys and not let them out unless you know what the hell their doing. They are costing you big time and it's your name that will go down in the history books as one of the worse Presidents. Stop campaigning and fund raising and start doing your job. I will be glad to come down and show you how.

Get your butt over to the useless department of education and give them some direction. Basics, do the basics, and teach all the children reading, writing, and arithmetic and don't forget penmanship. I'll be glad to go fix the problems there, just call.

June 6, 2013

President Barack Obama

1600 Pennsylvania Ave N.W.

Washington D.C. 20500

Dear President Obama,

And the beat goes on, what kind of headache medicine do you take? You have no one to blame but yourself. What do you care, your off fund raising. Comrades Xi and Obama are meeting in the California Desert, how appropriate, keep the news media as far away as you can. Good idea, they are not happy with you lately and you may not be invited to the press dinner next year.

The Patriot Act was instituted to gather information on suspected terrorist not the entire population of the United States. In case you forgot, they are usually from the Middle East and of Islamic persuasion, something you are familiar with. Now you do have a criminal element to watch out for, but that is not what the Patriot Act is all about. You donkeys are like a kid in the candy store, your never happy with one piece of candy. Now you have the gall to support your stupidity, not a good move.

Military aid to Egypt, did Kerry fall off the ketchup shelf and hit his head. What could they have promised us to get 1.3 billion in military aid? They don't like us and they said they don't like us, so what part of that don't you understand. Maybe it is time for America to mind its own business and concentrate on its own business.

So it's screw the students time, double the interest rate so they can't pay the loans off and use the IRS to collect the money when they can't pay, claiming they are government backed loans. The students get an education but not a job, the banks collect the interest, and the colleges get rich and waste the money on bloated professors that is a good formula for success.

Here is a good formula, give loans for zero interest and tell the colleges what they can charge, just like you cut the fees for doctors. The education system needs a bailout.

June 7, 2013

Presidents Barack Obama

1600 Pennsylvania Avenue N.W.

Washington D.C. 20500

Dear President Obama,

You are in California spreading rumors about Obamascare and you don't even know if will work, but you're not alone, I don't think anyone knows if is going to work. I haven't heard two people agree on the intended results other then it may end up to be a train wreck. You stated it may hit a few bumps in the road, but I think they will be sink holes. You are rolling the dice on premium hikes and if you don't make the point you will finish off the economy that hasn't recovered. There are still millions of people unemployed and that doesn't point to a recovery. The less said and the more managed is better but that is not your style.

National security concerns and the Patriot Act are not intended for monitoring grandmas' conversation. Like everything else the government does, they mess it up. You do not have a problem with the masses just the terrorists. The profile of a terrorist hasn't changed much since 911. I think you are gathering this information and using it for your party's advantage. I wonder how you missed any information on Benghazi or was someone asleep at the switch. There is no justification for all this information gathering. You are supposed to spy on the enemy, but if you are Islamic, everyone is your enemy????

Meeting with Xi from China, that is a good thing, one spy to another. I suggest you ask him how they financed the great wall maybe that will remind you of my suggestion for a national lottery with no federal tax for the winners and no one winning more than a million dollars. There is something you could be assured it will work and produce the results you want, just don't let Gruber get his hands on it.

It is appropriate that Xi meet with you in California, the land of the worst air pollution in this country. He probably feels right at home.

June 8, 2013

President Barack Obama

1600 Pennsylvania Avenue N.W.

Washington D.C. 20500

Dear President Obama,

The Obamascare success formula is taking control very soon, so let me share my calculations with you and see what that does for the health industry.

We have more doctors leaving private practice

We have more doctors refusing Medicare and private insurance

Individuals can't buy catastrophe insurance because they must follow Obamascare

Healthy people over 40 will have to take a more costly plan

More patients and less doctors equals longer appointment intervals

Young healthy people have to pay a higher premium for the basic plan

Small business implementation is delayed because the IRS states it's complicated

You are spending 54 million dollars for NAVIGATORS

People with preexisting conditions are being denied because the plan is short $$

There is no plan in place to replace short falls in medical staffing

Cutting doctors' fees and adding paperwork

And on and on and on and the IRS is controlling the success of Obamascare

This obviously is a formula for failure. You are taking more money away from the average family, which gives them less discretionary money, the medical profession has less money, less money equals a slower economy and how do you cover the 27 million people that are out of work. What employer do you fine and how do you fine the unemployed when they have no money to buy Obamascare.

I have the answer, pat Xi on the shoulder, whisper in his ear, make sure the microphones are off, and the media is out of the room and borrow a few trillion dollars until you leave the Whitehouse in three years. You can stick it to the next donkey.

June 9, 2013

President Barack Obama

1600 Pennsylvania Avenue N.W.

Washington D.C. 20500

Dear President Obama,

When I read the papers and the stories on line, it is becoming a real stretch to believe what I am reading, for instance;

Military not allowed to read about your scandals

Cancer patients forced into hospitals for treatment because of sequester cuts

Snooping that has gone beyond intention in the name of national security

Interruption in the normal course of business because of different political views

Lying, mismanagement and fraud at every government level

Incompetence in every facet of your administration and countless other stories

Worst of all, you have Bill Clinton made at you again, like you really care

Obamascare is a mess, the sequester deal you sponsored has backfired on you, you lost billions on your energy programs and GM, you increased the deficit, our troops are dying to promote Islam and not democracy, your disregard for the Constitution is blatant, and the list goes on. Exactly when are you going to start being an American for America and start doing your job????

Let me be fair, my disdain for you, the donkeys and the elephants has gone far beyond what I ever imagined would ever happen. The egotistical focus of you and the political parties is destroying this country and everything it stands for. There is a major flaw in your plan to socialize the country and control the duped media. Sooner than later, the money will run out and the poor and misinformed people you have been subsidizing will turn on you. It has already started at the managed level of government. People will not take the blame and cover up for the incompetence of you and the donkeys, but what do you care, you will walk away clean, MAYBE!

June 10, 2013

President Barack Obama

1600 Pennsylvania Avenue N.W.

Washington D.C. 20500

Dear President Obama,

I can't believe you are lending money to nonprofit insurance companies to compete with existing health insurance companies. It take profit to pay a loan back and keep companies afloat in the hard times. What will you do when this happens, loan them some more money? Obamascare has as much success as you playing par at the US Open. The Fisker Auto deal and Solyndra haven't taught you anything?

We are pass the realm of good intention sliding into a pit of stupidity. You need to add practicality to your staff, not a bunch of liberal professors who teach but can't do. There are still 27 million people that are unemployed, where is their solution for this. The solution is simple, fix the tax code for individuals and business, and put people in place that can streamline the government and make it more productive and stop the squandering of money. You need business people for that not political appointees.

The immigration bill comes up for a vote so they can debate the issues. Reid states he doesn't want major changes to the bill. Who died and left him boss? The simple solution is to secure the borders first. After you get that right, find the illegal immigrants and give them a choice of following a legitimate path to legalization or going home. This should be easy as you are snooping on everyone anyway. Enforce the current laws on the books and tell them to get over the fact they might have to prove citizenship if they are stopped. I had to do that for my license, passport school, and many other legal functions. This goes for everyone coming into the country, especially people that have religious and political views that threaten are national security, and just so you know there are people that don't like us so get over it.

June 11, 2013

President Barack Obama

1600 Pennsylvania Avenue N.W.

Washington D.C. 20500

Dear President Obama,

What part of the Constitution doesn't Biden understand? I'll tell you, nothing. How can he criticize Paul and Cruz for their actions when he is one of the banditos who has voted this country into debt and fiscal uncertainty? Why are you and him out fund raising? That was not part of your oath of office. So when are you going to China?

Who is the genius that hired Snowden and put him in a sensitive position to expose your information gathering? Your administration doesn't have to be transparent, it's full of snitches and rats and none of them like what you and the donkeys are doing to the country. With all that is going on, I would be embarrassed if I were a real donkey watching blunder after blunder.

This makes a great headline by Clapper, "I gave the least untruth," about what it doesn't matter, a lie is a lie, have a lollypop and go to bed, and better yet you're in timeout for stupidity. How can anyone in Washington think they will get away with a lie or half-truth, when they have hundreds of reports looking for a headline? Remember, you pissed off the press, now nothing is sacred.

Well Illinois hasn't passed Obamascare, the state noted for dirty politics and backstabbing is doing to one of their own, how appropriate. I gave you some great advice and told you to start over and have the medical field, not the drug lords, help you write a feasible bill. We won't have any time to deal with the real issues, like jobs and the economy, the congress will be too busy trying to fix Obamascare. You couldn't institute it one step at a time and do it right, so now you have a cluster pluck. Sebelius, Holder, Snowden, Clapper, The IRS, Obamascare, and the hit keep coming, keep ducking.

June 12, 2013

President Barack Obama

1600 Pennsylvania Avenue N.W.

Washington D.C. 20500

Dear President Obama,

I have a major problem with the amount of time you spend fund raising. This is not in your job description and does nothing to help America other that support your party. If you must continue to do this do it on your dime or have the DNC pay for all the support and expenses. You are out of control and by this I mean once is too often.

More and more information is coming out about doctor shortages and doctors leaving the Medicare and Medicaid program. Knowing how big your administration is on classified leaks, I wonder if any of this information has leaked your way. What is your solution to this problem? Also, cutting doctor fees is not the way you to keep them in the program. Doctor Nathan Fink had a great idea to help Medicare expenses, put a copay on all second opinion doctor visits. If you investigate this you will probably find measurable abuses, this should also be done for people that abuse emergency room visits and we know that is being done.

Maybe some of the information you gather should support the economic crisis we are going through and the fact that 27 million people are out of work. Maybe you can catch the people that are abusing the entitlement programs and prosecute them with this information. The 2 billion dollar complex in Utah should be used to help you solve some of the domestic problems and keep America free. As they say on Wall Street, information is everything, they seem to know how to use it better than your administration.

The immigration bill is full of Constitutional challenges. It appears like the entire bill is designed around increasing the democratic vote, but falls short when it comes to where the money will come from for changes that will occur. The bill is a sham and a cover for the inefficient controls we have in place now. Don't sign it.

June 13, 2013

President Barack Obama

1600 Pennsylvania Avenue N.W.

Washington D.C. 20500

Dear President Obama,

Stop and Frisk, what's the problem? I have to show my ID at the bank, at the doctor's office, at the airport, at the grocery store, at the military base I visit and many other places. So, what's the big deal? The big deal is this, the failure of your administration and other administrations to deliver the promises they made to low income Americans. So why shouldn't the police be suspicious if they are not a regular in the neighborhood. You have ignored their plight and made them more reliant because of the liberal entitlements you give them, but it's never enough. The government has wasted billions on green programs and bailing out GM and hasn't spent a dime educating and training the low income earners to better themselves. Encouraging speeches and appearances are not as good as hands on education and training. I believe it is the goal of the government to keep them in their situation and dependent. Instead of importing talent from other countries, there just may be talent among this group that need a boost.

The senate has failed to pass the border protection section of the immigration bill, well that's a real revelation, fighting over votes rather than protecting America. Stupid. This failure has caused the need for this legislation and now it is compounding the problem. What message are we sending to people who risk their lives trying to come here? What part of this doesn't government understand, we need to get control of the people that are here illegally, root out the good and the bad, qualify them for citizenship, and send the trouble makers and gang members back. The lack of support by government officials is the problem and the donkey program to swell the democratic voting ranks, after all that's what this is really about, elections.

It is amazing, the FBI director doesn't know who is leading the IRS investigation?

June 14, 2013

President Barack Obama

1600 Pennsylvania Avenue N.W.

Washington D.C. 20500

Dear President Obama,

Well it's time to give you an at a boy, putting the federal employees on Obamascare is the right thing to do, and this should include the senate and the congress. They can try to maneuver around this all they want and send you legislation to counter this, but don't sign the bill. If they over ride your veto, then they have signed their own pink slip.

Helping Syria is the right thing to do, a day late and a dollar short. I know the election had something to do with this late decision, after all, what was more important, you getting elected or saving the lives of men, women, and children in Syria. Politics is a heartless game even though the donkeys are the feel good party, they are the only ones who want to feel good. Anyway, about time and it is about time you bring home the troops and stop screwing the veterans with medical and financial support.

I mentioned in previous letters that you should start a practical support group that could help during national disasters. You can recruit these people from released veterans, the unemployed, especially the low income and talented Americans, and select specialist that could help train them. They should be trained in all aspects of disaster relief, security, firefighting, flood, wind, tornado and storm rescue. These would be hands on workers that would help people rebuild and move on with their lives. Their job wouldn't be done until the community was functional again and the insurance companies would have to help support and pay their share. The people and the insurance companies would be happy if only ten homes burned instead of over 400. This is doable and a job creator, not one of your strong points. Think of America first.

I don't know if your best job is being a father, your never home!

June 15, 2013

President Barack Obama

1600 Pennsylvania Avenue N.W.

Washington D.C. 20500

Dear President Obama,

Wouldn't it be cheaper to fly the people you need to see in Africa than to spend millions going over there? How do you justify this expense and for that matter all the travel expense of the congress and senate. Seems a bit overboard to me.

Your comment about sexual assault in the military is in the headlines. Too bad they don't hold your feet to the fire for all the promises you make. Congress seems to be a very selective group when it comes to taking the blame and pointing the blame. You sure have had your fair share of finger pointing. I guess that's why you make the big bucks, right.

Obamascare is scaring everyone especially the congress. They must be beside themselves, thinking they might have to be part of a medical plan that is good for everyone else and not them. Maybe they should have read the bill before they voted on it. Thirty seven votes by the house to recall it, what a waste of time, money and paper. I hope you don't use this as a bargaining chip when it comes time and sell Americans down the road. Compliance for everyone is the right thing to do.

It would be a great idea if we knew what reward was on the other end of sending weapons to Syria. I would like assurances that the population will be protected if the rebels achieve power and that America will not become their next rhetorical target and side with the rest of the extremist. Do we really know who is in charge over there? Egypt should have taught us that lesson. All aid should be cut off from them. I guess we deserve what we get since we didn't react because the donkeys wanted you reelected.

Listen, forget about it, have a Happy Father's Day.

June 16, 2013

President Barack Obama

1600 Pennsylvania Avenue N.W.

Washington D.C. 20500

Dear President Obama,

What happens when you rush the job you are doing? Sooner or later something will happen and it won't be good. The premium hikes that Obamascare will cause is going to cost the donkey's big time. You are lucky that there is an election before Obamascare takes full effect. Health insurance premiums have been going up as long as I can remember, so who were the geniuses who thought Obamascare was going to lower premiums or keep them in check? Too much, too fast, too complicated and too expensive, a real formula for failure. You should have read the bill, too late.

You are going to the peace talks. Are you going to bring your Nobel Peace Medal and say, I'm the winner, you have to listen to me. How can you solve world conflict when half of you want to fight and the other half want weapons and money to fight with? It is cheaper to get rid of the leaders and start over than killing the population and having massive health issues. Peace will exist, when governments mind their own business and treat their people fairly, that doesn't mean you should give them a lollypop every time they cry, like we do in America. People and government have to earn respect together.

The gay rights issue is all about benefits and money, not about how people feel about each other. A blessing and a marriage certificate is not a bonding agent forever, your divorce rate indicates that. It is all about benefits and money. People should get what they are entitled to from the government, not live off of someone else's contributions. The last time I looked, the Constitution didn't mention anything about marriage, just individual rights. Government has failed to consider individual rights when it comes to entitlements. Everyone should contribute if everyone wants to receive, with exceptions.

June 17, 2013

President Barack Obama

1600 Pennsylvania Avenue N.W.

Washington D.C. 20500

Dear President Obama,

It makes a pretty picture, you and Putin sitting together, He supplies Syria weapons to kill the population and you supply weapons to the people to kill the government. The result is less people and less government and you guys talk peace. You just can't make this stuff up, two peace loving countries supplying the rest of the world with weapons to kill each other. Why don't you agree to stop supplying weapons to anyone, makes sense to me.

Your approval rating is tanking, not that you care. You will still be President for three more years and maybe you will help lose more seats in the house and senate. That is a good achievement, less donkeys and more elephants, so we will think more and feel less and still get nothing done.

If you are really counting on the young population to make Obamascare successful, then you must believe in the tooth fairy too. If they have jobs they won't be able to afford health care and student loans. Something will have to go and since health care doesn't affect their credit rating, it will be a simple choice. Jobs are what people need so they can work hard and get sick and be covered by their employer, unless the employer hires immigrants, no Obamascare for 13 years and no fine. Sounds like a success formula for the youth of America. Maybe they can enter the new field for attorneys, interpreting Obamascare.

According to the Supreme Court, you don't need to prove citizenship to vote in the federal elections, so why don't we mail out absentee ballots to the rest of the world and they can decide our next election. We give them our money, why not the right to vote.

June 18, 2013

President Barack Obama

1600 Pennsylvania Avenue N.W.

Washington D.C. 20500

Dear President Obama,

La t da, congress passed a bill making abortion illegal after 20 weeks of pregnancy. That took a real stroke of genius. This is amazing, a government that decides when it is ok to kill and not ok to kill. The issue is a personal and individual problem, not a government problem. It is a woman's choice and that is ok, but 20 weeks, it seems like there needs to be a tighter limit and quicker decision process.

Another issue is a person right to die if they are verified terminally ill. While congress is determining when babies, through proxy, have the right to die, what about sick people. Everyone should have the right to a dignified death under these circumstances. Congress needs to get on the same page for everyone.

The G8 turned out to be a real success, they agreed to disagree and solved nothing. I know they can't do this by email, you never know where that message will wind up, but they could call and just state, they haven't changed their position and saved the tax payers money. What a waste of time and money.

Please explain to me why the federal government pays out bonuses? They push paper and waste money doing it. They have a job and they are compensated for doing it, end of pay check. The notion that you will not get quality people if you don't pay a bonus doesn't set well when you have 27 million people unemployed. They have a generous pension plan, a generous health care plan, and steady work, not to mention the benefits and time off. You can't state that everyone is part of the fraud and waste they allow though their inefficient work, but show me 100% efficiency and no waste for the pay they receive. What can Americans expect when government workers have congress and the senate as examples, and don't forget the golfer?

June 19, 2013

President Barack Obama

1600 Pennsylvania Avenue N.W.

Washington D.C. 20500

Dear President Obama,

I mentioned to you long ago to repeal Obamascare and start again. Well, according to you administration, they are not ready to implement the program because of data shortage. What a surprise, I guess you weren't monitoring the right information. The health plan is on its way to dismal failure. Why, because improving it in small and decisive steps isn't good enough, it had to be all or nothing. I am afraid for the people because that is what they will have, nothing. This will hurt the economy, health care, and the people, but that is what this is all about, people depending on the government control.

Animals have more respect for their young than people do, but to be fair, they don't have the government mandating a death sentence. With all that is available over the counter, why do we need a bill sentencing children to life or death? Moral values are not government issued like military gear. It starts at the home with two parents and a strong family environment. It is difficult to develop any of that when you have high unemployment, liberal entitlement programs, and limited consequences for the person who fractures the family. Maybe we need a happy pill so people will stay married and support the family value. No, we already have marijuana and that's not working. I wonder if anyone investigated marijuana's cancer causing effects.

The immigration bill is as bad as Obamascare, trying to do it all at one time. How can we register these illegals and ask them to pay taxes and a fine when most of them don't have a job. How can we justify giving them jobs when we have 27 million unemployed? Secure the borders, deal with the illegal registration, deal with the entitlement programs that make the people reliant on a fractured government, and push education in the skilled and unskilled industries. Working people are happy people.

June 20, 2013

President Barack Obama

1600 Pennsylvania Avenue N.W.

Washington D.C. 20500

Dear President Obama,

Sometimes you are dumber than your donkey mascot. The only thing divisive about faith base education is the fact the children are better educated. The divisiveness comes from the parents that are like you, you think your way is better than anyone else's. I am sure the donkey thinks that way too, maybe not, they all seem to get along. Your Islamic approach is ridiculous. Maybe you need a new speech writer.

What is the point of going to Ireland and starting trouble between the religious bases? I think I know, it must have something to do with Islamic supremacy, and their lust to conquer the world. We don't have enough problems at home for you to worry about, so you add fuel to the fire somewhere else.

Do something I can give you credit for, like make a deal with keystone for a fixed low gas price for your approval. This will help the poor and middle class and give a boost to the economy and jobs. This is a single dimension thought process which is hard for you to comprehend. Simple, guarantee the country a $2.50 per gallon gas price for X number of years, minimal export, and no outsourcing beyond Canada and the U.S. and you can approve the bill. This will help the environmentalist also, it won't cost them so much to travel around the world starting trouble. Some of their efforts are noble and some just plain stupid.

The food stamp program needs to be revised and I have suggested it before. Have Michelle establish a list of products that can be purchased with food stamps and have the manufactures code the products. Maybe the children will start getting the intended use of the program and won't go to school or be home hungry. No drug test, no food stamps.

June 21, 2013

President Barack Obama

1600 Pennsylvania Avenue N.W.

Washington D.C. 20500

Dear President Obama,

I know you can't know everything that goes on in government but it seems like more goes on behind your back than you are aware of. The problem with this is these problems don't take care of themselves, they just become bigger problems. I don't believe everything I read, but you must admit, how you can make up some of these stories. The latest example is the IRS sending forty six million dollars in refunds to the same address, can this really be true. It probably is and you will never know about it because you are layered away. The other problem is you never visit these agencies and set your standard. There are too many small incidents that add up to major incidents.

You are living the high life right now and I don't expect you to understand what the average American has to go through on a daily basis. You and your speech writers feel the pain of the average person, but that is on paper only. When is the last time you filled up your gas tank or paid an electric bill? Why don't you going shopping once a month and see the real cost of food and pay for it. In business high volume or sales hides a multitude of sins in operating a business. You don't really see the impact until the sales go down and then the waste and mismanagement jump off the profit and loss statements.

Everything will start to change as the fed pulls back on the bond buying. You're lucky, they will wean the economy off the excessive money flow and then the mismanagement and waste in government will magnify and the demand for more taxes will slide off your lips and fill the air, not that hasn't happened already. The worst is yet to come, but I thing good business practices will help bail you out. Obamascare will not help you and that is your Achilles Heel. You better see a doctor!

June 22, 2013

President Barack Obama

1600 Pennsylvania Avenue N.W.

Washington D.C. 20500

Dear President Obama,

The Keystone people must be pretty stupid if they are depending on you to approve the pipeline when you are making climate change one of your major efforts in the next three years. It is a noble undertaking but not very smart. How will you get other countries like China to participate? What edge do you have over them to make them come to the table, I'll tell you, none, but here is a hint, buy less products from China and other Asian nations and you will have less pollution. The buyers should set the standards but that will never happen because they are profit driven. Look at the clothes manufactures and what the companies that buy their products have done to workers and the conditions they work in, deplorable. If you can change the profit mindset of companies, maybe you stand a chance for climate change. Good luck and stop putting everything on the Americans back.

The farm bill is a joke. The food stamp program is out of control and the gas prices are a major economic problem. I stated in my past letters, you control the energy prices you will have a good economy. The lower class will have stronger buying and maybe investing power. Food prices will go down and food sales will go up driving food cost lower. Climate change will be an added cost to everything right now. You need to get the cause under control before you can fix the problem. Your donkeys are on the wrong side of the wagon that has no wheels.

I know I make prospective solutions sound easy and they are if you focus on one thing at a time. What problem have you fixed since you been in office? I can't think of any. Talking about solutions is like me writing these letters, it goes nowhere but it makes me feel better and I am sure you feel better after your speeches.

June 23, 2013

President Barack Obama

1600 Pennsylvania Avenue N.W.

Washington D.C. 20500

Dear President Obama,

If the farm bill doesn't go down in flames, you should veto it. The food stamp program doesn't belong with the farm bill. The subsidies to corporate farms should not be a profit builder and that bill should stand alone. I hope we are not giving tobacco farms any money. That is like two slaps in the face. The farmers who need help should get help and the major corporations should get audits.

It is pretty stupid on people's part to think the government is not looking over their shoulder. I always stated that if you don't want people to know your business, then don't talk about it. What is private about anyone's life you can't find on the internet or in the newspaper? Besides the electronic surveillance, you need more boots on the ground in hostile countries. If the bad guys don't think your monitoring their calls and activity, then they are stupid also. Keeping America safe is the first priority and mending people's feelings because your snooping is low on the list when it comes to homeland security.

Have you asked Michelle to work on the food stamp program as I suggested? What are you waiting for? There is a big savings there and maybe the food will go the children and the needy as intended. Don't ask the food manufactures to cooperate, tell them, your good at that and Michelle will get the desired results. I am sure she will do a much better job with this than Hillary did with health care. Don't blow up the budget doing this, it is supposed to save money and narrow the intended target, Michelle can be extravagant. She needs to stay home as well as you and save the money so we can have tours of the Whitehouse again. It is only your residence, not your house.

June 24, 2013

President Barack Obama

1600 Pennsylvania Avenue N.W.

Washington D.C. 20500

Dear President Obama,

Why are Muslims, unions and other select groups exempt from Obamascare? If it is good for one person in America then it is good for all, including you. You are the most prejudice president that has ever served. The only thing you care about is the moment and appearance. You are and will always be the flimflam man in my book. You do what in necessary to make you look good or keep you out of trouble. I stated before, you need to send Obamascare to the crapper and start over again. If there were a law against stupidity, you and the people that voted for Obamascare would be on the most wanted list.

Sending troops to Egypt and giving them over a billion dollars in military and financial aid is dumb. They are not our friends and some day they will use your generosity against us. You are using our money to further a cause that wants America destroyed and there is no way to cover that up. It is obvious that people that never worked in the private sector for what they have are the first people who want to give our origin of wealth away.

You and your administration let Snowden get away and now you look like the donkey's ass. This man will cause you irreparable damage, not that you don't do that on your own, and has grabbed the headline from you. Your so called friend in other countries don't want to give him up because he exposed something they already knew. They are taking advantage of you and there isn't anything you can do about. Maybe they will isolate him enough for you to send a drone after him. Be brave and tell the 100,000 people who signed the petition for his pardon, you don't pardon traitors.

June 25, 2013

President Barack Obama

1600 Pennsylvania Avenue N.W.

Washington D.C. 20500

Dear President Obama,

Man get off the fence! How can you approve the pipeline in Oklahoma and sit on the fence for the rest of the project. Make a deal and get on with it. Stop being a girly man. Get the guarantees you want and set your sights on completion.

Tell Harry to shut up. He makes the donkey look smarter than him. Who did he think the reporter was talking to if he was the only man standing there? It is dog track time for him.

Only citizens should be entitled to government benefits. If people are not willing to become a citizen, then they are only here for the money and the life style. No benefits of any kind should be afforded to them. They should declare their intentions when they come to the country. They should agree to the requirements upon entry and their progress followed. If they fail to meet the requirements, they go home.

I am tired of listening to people that add a prefix to American. If you were born here then you are an American, not Italian, black, Spanish, Asian or Indian, just American. If you love your heritage so much, then go there and live, otherwise shut up.

A president that is concerned with climate change as you are, should stay home and stop adding to the problem, stop flying all over the world. Let your fingers do the walking. It will better serve the climate if leaders who travel with less came here.

Have you addressed the problem with the IRS for sending 46 million dollars to the same address in refunds? Probably not, the sum is too meager for you to get involved, but someone has to set the standard and you are not doing that. I haven't seen you call anyone to the Whitehouse for answers to these scandals and gross mismanagement.

Why are Muslins exempt from Obamascare?

June 26, 2013

President Barack Obama

1600 Pennsylvania Avenue N.W.

Washington D.C. 20500

Dear President Obama,

DOMA went down for the count and was declared unconstitutional. What is unconstitutional is the people that collect federal benefits that have never contributed. There isn't means testing when benefits are awarded to drug addicts and alcoholics. There are no limits or qualifications for people that stay on the dole as life support. The efforts of the government to rehabilitate remove people from support id lacking or nonexistent. So, now the Supreme Court has put another financial burden on business and the government and the people that will pay are the working people. They will get a double whammy, more taxes and the cost increases companies will have to do to cover these additional benefits. DOMA has made the cost of doing business more costly as well as Obamascare. Economically Stupid.

Sending the VRA to the grave is the right thing to do in this day and age. This is a problem that can be handled by the Justice Department the same way they handled the interference by thugs blocking and intimidating voters. The federal government and not the states have hand cuffed the people with their uncontrollable entitlement programs. People are not going to vote against their source of income and the donkeys use this as a weapon against these Americans. Most Americans vote their pocketbook and the Hollywood image of the candidate.

It is about time you go to the IRS building and kick some butt. That organization is out of control and heads need to role, not be put on paid suspension. The managers are allowing the workers to run wild without retribution. Show some leadership while you are in the country and set an example. Are you part of the problem or the solution?

June 27, 2013

President Barack Obama

1600 Pennsylvania Avenue N.W.

Washington D.C. 20500

Dear President Obama,

Why is Bin Bayyah, meeting with Whitehouse officials and the NSA???? The man is a known terrorist and hates America. Send him home. He is not going to tell or convince any of his followers to love America. This muslin program for world domination isn't in anyone's best interest. Don't try to tell me you're investigating him when it amounts to simply sleeping with the enemy. It is bad enough you have family ties to the Muslin world and you are a socialist that endorses government control, we don't need this man's face in our business. This is like the Vietnam War, you can't tell the good guys from the bad, so send them all packing.

When are you going to the IRS and kick some butt? Maybe, you can't recognize the problem because your administration operates the same way. The SWAG method, scientific wild ass guess, is not the preferred method of running the government, but it seems like your preferred method. Give up a golf date and go to the IRS and do what has to be done.

Boehner is not moving on the senate's version of the immigration bill. Is he indicating the 435 house members are smarter than the 100 senators? Once he passes the house version it will go to conference where a small group will demonstrate how smart they are and how dumb 535 members of the house and senate are. What a waste of time and money!

The bottom line to this whole thing is if you don't like it, you will veto it. So the question is which gems from the donkey organization do you have influencing the house and senate? We know it is all about getting votes and making them dependent on the government.

June 28, 2013

President Barack Obama

1600 Pennsylvania Avenue N.W.

Washington D.C. 20500

Dear President Obama,

It is very clear, the only people benefiting from Obamascare, are the lawyers. The ACA has generated numerous cases in the courts and will continue to do so. As much as Obamascare will hurt the economy, it will make the rich richer and the poor poorer. Business owners will suffer and so will the people who don't want to participate. What people don't understand, is that the IRS will use its powers to make sure all the fines are paid by individuals and business. You still have time to dump this mess.

It is very sad when you have to pay children and silicate help from the NFL and other organizations to promote Obamascare. The bottom line to this program is it won't work unless you have all the young people on it. How can they afford it when you and congress allowed the student loan rates to double? This is a dumb move and when the young people finally wake up to what you are doing to them, they will riot all over this country. Businesses will not tolerate having to pay family rates for students until they are 26 years old. The lawyers will find a way around that.

When will all federal employees be put on Obamascare? When the people start hurting in the pocket and see they are not equals, but subservient to the government, you will finish your journey to becoming the worse President this country ever had. Your ego will survive this because you can always say they elected me twice, how stupid were they.

You are on the go again with the family, is this an official business trip. Let's chalk it up that way and add it to the government waste we already have. These millions, for the trip, are a tear drop to the billions we already waste and do nothing about. The information and gifts you collect will help fill up your library.

June 29, 2013

President Barack Obama

1600 Pennsylvania Avenue N.W.

Washington D.C. 20500

Dear President Obama,

Helping other nations when you are in a position to do it is great, we are not. It doesn't surprise me that GE will be part of this power solution for Africa. I wonder what is more important, food and medicine or paying an electric bill. It is very generous of you to give away what we don't have.

At home the students will be facing double interest rates on their loans for college. I see you only devoted limited time and effort toward solving that problem. You tell the youth of Africa that they need to carry the torch toward success and you have the youth in America owing over a trillion dollars in debt. How does that equate in your mind and what have you done about congress forgiving school debt for their federal staffers. Did you have a college loan and pay it back???

The Department of Education will spend over 77 billion dollars in discretionary spending for education and not be responsible for educating anyone. What a waste of money. I wonder how many free colleges we could have for that money. I'm no expert, but it seems like more than one, and just think, illegals can go there too.

It is difficult for me to comprehend you telling the Africans how to do things when we have so many problem here. I don't see any positive feedback from this trip or you learning anything that will benefit America. If the trip costs about 100 million dollars, I consider it a waste of money when a phone call could have done the same thing. You set a great example for others when our country has high unemployment, massive waste in government, a congress and senate that can't get it right, and you, a lost leader. Maybe we should just consider this trip as discretionary spending!

June 30, 2013

President Barack Obama

1600 Pennsylvania Avenue N.W.

Washington D.C. 20500

Dear President Obama,

Desmond Tutu sent you on your way with a heavy burden, peace in the Middle East and your success giving Africans a path to follow. So far, you are a disappointment on both counts. The biggest disappointment is the condition and scandals in our own country and your lack of attention to them. Desmond Tutu is wrong, you came from your home and you are returning to your home and you are a role model that is tarnished by your lack of leadership. You should look at their accomplishments and try to exceed to their level.

I stated several times about a national disaster team and the necessary equipment to help people in distress. We lost 19 firemen in Arizona, maybe if a plane was available to drop retardant on short notice, some may have survived.

I hope you noticed on your trip the difference that Desmond Tutu makes with the funds he has available and the waste and mismanagement in our government. You don't make it a priority, it will never get done. Government waste is out of control and so it congresses entitlements and spending. Someone has to make it a priority and move the government to an efficient level. Adding 135,000 employees is not the answer.

Desmond Tutu was right in asking you to step up to the plate and give young Africans a boost to their psyche, but wrong thinking you are your own man. He is not considering your loyalty to the donkey brigade and their agenda to keep the poor and the middle class under their entitlement thumbs. You have a high mountain to climb and there isn't much oxygen at the top to keep you going. Regardless of that, the real challenge is do you want to do it???

July 1, 2013

President Barack Obama

1600 Pennsylvania Avenue N.W.

Washington D.C. 20500

Dear President Obama,

We spy on our allies and enemies and they have their nose out of joint, too bad. They do the same to us, only, they don't have some jerk advertising it all over the world. It makes you look bad and is a point of contention when negotiating, but tell them to get over it. At the same time you can tell all these privacy hawks to settle their feathers and calm their hormones, there is nothing private in this world or space in this world.

All these jerks that want to get on drugs and legalized marijuana should be taxed into oblivion. They are the direct and indirect cause of many innocent deaths in the drug supply network just so they can enjoy running away from life for a while. You need to follow the federal law and crack down on the users with stiffer penalties and jail time. The problem is out of hand and needs to be addressed.

I hope you are enjoying your trip back in time. Maybe it will give you some insight into helping the children in America that are disadvantaged because they are being depressed by the donkeys and the elephants. Where is their incentive to progress when you have them waiting for the government check every month? This has become an epidemic on all levels. It is time for solutions not handouts. Better and longer education without the option of quitting is the answer. Special boot camps for the attitudes is the answer for disciplinary students. No time to play, no time to get in trouble.

I know you can't be thinking of that disaster program I wrote about, because you are reminiscing about the past in Africa. Looking back is not the answer, you see the mistakes that were made then and you think you can do a better job repeating history. History is for books and libraries, not for shakers and movers. Time to go back to work!!!

July 2, 2013

President Barack Obama

1600 Pennsylvania Avenue N.W.

Washington D.C. 20500

Dear President Obama,

Obamascare is turning into a real cluster pluk. Now you are delaying a program that should have been scrapped in the first place. The IRS keeps adding new regulations to a program they can't figure out. They are looking for the right foot to fit the shoe and not the shoe to fit the foot. This is great, a program that has so many problems and hasn't even begun. This is what you get for signing something you didn't read, not that it would have mattered because the donkeys wanted it.

I guess that peace medal you received is becoming a curse and not an award. They don't want peace in the Middle East. The Islamic hard core want world domination. I thought I would mention that in case you missed it. Now the Islamic leaders are telling their people to do what it takes to stop the Olympic game in Russia. Big mistake on their part, because the Russians will just shoot them. I still don't hear much from the peaceful Islamic movement, probably because there isn't one.

Get rid of Clapper, what does he understand if he didn't understand the question put to him about spying? Isn't that what the NSA does, spies on people. What does he think he is, the editor of People Magazine? His adversaries and counter parts must think he is dumber than a stick, at least a stick can find water.

I can understand why Michelle likes to take trips on the taxpayer's dime, she thinks she lives in a beautiful prison. It doesn't seem to bother you too much, you still play golf, an occasional basketball game and you are away from the beautiful prison very often. I can't imagine that hardship, working from home when you are at home. Don't worry, you only have about 3.5 years left to serve and I'm glad it's not a lifetime.

July 3, 2013

President Barack Obama

1600 Pennsylvania Avenue N.W.

Washington D.C. 20500

Dear President Obama,

The projected problems with Obamascare are out of control. You would think by now, you would have a competent committee review the bill you signed and offer suggestions, even if is to start over again and go step by step. In light of the fact, the IRS is a dysfunctional agency, changing them would be a step toward progress. You need to do what is right for America, not the donkeys. The ACA will be remembered as Obamascare, not donkey doo, and will be the cross your name will bare forever.

I hope Morsi isn't going to abscond with the billion dollars Kerry promised them. It seems the people in Egypt have more brains than the state department. With all the spying that is being done, why didn't they see this coming? You need more boots on the ground gathering information then you need people with headsets and computers. Of course, you are partial to sharia law so you weren't about to help the young people seek democracy. They prevailed because they know they are facing a changing and challenging world. I salute the Egyptian people that understand independence is better than government control.

Now that you African trip is over, maybe you can do something about the student loan rates, you know, make a few calls, cut off their donkey funds for the 2014 election, or use some of the dirt you collected on the elephants to pass a good law. This will require you being in the office and not on the campaign trail raising money. I wonder where campaigning is covered in the Constitution after you take office. I don't recall it in the oath of office either. It must be in the donkey bylaws when you run for office, like in, help you brother donkey, donate a dollar today.

July 4, 2013

President Barack Obama

1600 Pennsylvania Avenue N.W.

Washington D.C. 20500

Dear President Obama,

I hope you had a happy Fourth of July. I always enjoy the nation's birthday and the fact I volunteered for the Marine Corp back in 1966, not my best experience in the beginning but overall I wouldn't trade it for anything. It is a momentous feeling when you are with your brothers under dangerous conditions. It is a true American feeling of dependency on each other and the independency of being an American. I wish I could have been there to help the Americans in Benghazi. You keep the spy network going for National security reasons and stop spying for the donkeys.

Thinking of Benghazi, the IRS, fast and furious, and Obamascare, when are you going to do something about it? You need to kick some butt and make some changes, it doesn't look good for you or your library wall.

The elephants and donkeys are have trouble over the voting rights act. The solution is simple, you prove you are an American citizen, you get to vote. If you can't read, write or speak English, then your credentials would be suspect. You need to prove this at the place where you vote, every time, not with a phony voting card, no proof no vote. This is not as harsh as it sound, we have to do it to get a driver's license in N.J.

So far you have stuck it to the medical profession, the college students, the poor and middle class, the military and many other facets of the American dream. I suggest you stick it to the donkeys, stay home, get some meaningful work done, fire the incompetents that are making you look like the donkey's butt, find out what the hell is going on with Obamascare, and be the President that the people elected you to be, The President of the United States of America, not the donkey party.

July 5, 2013

President Barack Obama

1600 Pennsylvania Avenue N.W.

Washington D.C. 20500

Dear President Obama,

I have enclosed a copy of my first book to you. The mail department has been reading my letters for over 200 days and the book contains my first one hundred and thirty letters. I wrote a thank you to the mail room on the last page and advised them you will continue to get these letters. I think you are a very good person, but I am not happy with your job performance and the way the donkeys manipulate you.

I write how I think and feel about what you do every morning. Most of the time I am puzzled by your decisions and inability to change course when necessary. I hope you enjoy reading it as much as I enjoyed writing it.

July 6, 2013

President Barack Obama

1600 Pennsylvania Avenue N.W.

Washington D.C. 20500

Dear President Obama,

The battle to raise the debt ceiling is coming up and the elephants are offering several different options for you to choose. It is criminal that we have to raise the debt ceiling in the first place, but I guess we must continue to pay for the mismanaged government and the poor decisions made in the past.

I don't understand how you can look for more money when you have a government of runaway fiscal management. I read reports if the waste, but I never see any solutions. You need to get on your pony and visit the different agencies and kick some fiscal butts. If you can't, fire your useless czars and hire people that can go in and do what is necessary. I question your support of a well-managed government.

You and the elephants and donkeys should start at a base line and set up mini cuts that will progress over the years to get spending under control. Without checking government waste and fraud, no matter what you do will not be enough. This needs to be done simultaneously to achieve a positive productive result. Look for people that can help you achieve this goal and move ahead.

Social security, the CPI, Medicaid, food stamps agricultural, military, education, and especially the expenses of congress should be adjusted in minor and progressive cuts that will not have major impact on the economy. Congress should face massive cuts in their expenses. The return on that investment is as dismal as their performance.

The student loan program is simple, charge an interest rate that is level with the expense of administration. Do not bloat these expenses, use people already in place and do not hire additional people to do this. Use the people in the education department that are doing less than they should be doing, which is close to nothing.

July 7, 2013

President Barack Obama

1600 Pennsylvania Avenue N.W.

Washington D.C. 20500

Dear President Obama,

Obamascare has been your cross to bear from day one and you will do nothing to come down from the cross. How can you justify closing the doors to the Whitehouse to the public and opening the bank at the Treasury Department to keep Obamascare from failing? This is total nonsense, providing money without verification of income, just so you can try and convince the young people to get insurance. This is not going to happen, young people think they are invincible and want to spend their discretionary money on good time and fun, not health insurance.

The waste and mismanagement in the government isn't bad enough, now you want to add this measure of stupidity. How do you justify delaying the business portion of Obamascare and moving ahead with the individual portion, it is unlawful? You are punishing the poor and middle class and making the insurance companies rich. What part of this don't you understand?

I stated this before and I will state it again, you need to get rid of the donkeys in your administration. They are making you look dumb and using you. Wake up! You are a great fund raiser and speaker, but a terrible analyst. I have heard more than one professional state that the people who give you advice need to go.

It is easy for me to give advice not being on the hot seat, but sometimes you see things better from far away. I mentioned the food stamp program several times. Michelle would be the perfect person to administer this program and make sure the children and adults received what they need to improve their health and survive. I hope you are not using this program as a bargaining chip for the debt ceiling debate that is coming up. I wouldn't put it pass the donkeys or elephant's to do such a thing.

Do something positive and non-controversial for the rest of your time in office. Your ideas are good but execution of the programs is disastrous. I hope you enjoy the book I sent with all good intentions.

July 8, 2013

President Barack Obama

1600 Pennsylvania Avenue N.W.

Washington D.C. 20500

Dear President Obama,

Your wait and see attitude on Egypt is going to put you on the wrong side again. Find a friend and support them if you are going to continue to waste the taxpayer's money. The Muslin Brotherhood was never a friend from the beginning and your state department should have known that, maybe they did and as usual you followed the donkey instead of your good judgment. I really wonder about that sometimes.

I warned you over and over again about moving too fast with Obamascare and here we are in a cluster pluk. Does anyone know what they are doing with Obamascare, besides wasting money? One step at a time, chip and deal, going all in will cost you in the short term. Cover the preexisting conditions and give yourself time to revise the rest of the program, but put someone in charge that knows what the hell their doing. Backing up is not losing, just a tactical maneuver.

I see you are meeting with the black caucus, what part of being American don't they understand. Are there problems any different than any other American in their situation? Family values and education are the strong roots for success. These failures don't have color barriers and the sooner Americans understand that the better off the country will be. There will always be prejudice in people's personal lives, but never in business. The cream will always rise to the top no matter who you are or what you look like. It is strange in times of disaster, how we all work together and when it's over most forget the Americans that helped. It did not matter at the time who you were or what you looked like and it should never matter.

The illusion that really matters, is what matters to you? You talk the talk, but you never walk it thru to success. The people you rely on are not delivering the results and always going back to the bank, thinking throwing more money at the obstacles will remove them. You are a jack of all trades and a master of none. If you are ever going to be a master at any trade, let it be the ability to select the right person for the right job.

July 9, 2013

President Barack Obama

1600 Pennsylvania Avenue N.W.

Washington D.C. 20500

Dear President Obama,

Definitely, bring the troops home. Let them choose their own form of government and live their own way. They will never be a democracy as long as sharia law is the base of their constitution. There are too many interpretations of the law just as there is of the Bible. Society will take over as the world progress thru the information network. I don't believe they want to improve their country and move forward. BRING THE TROOPS HOME and concentrate on protecting America.

I would hate to think the train wreck had anything to do with the Keystone pipeline, but we have had similar accidents in this country. I would rather clean up a spill instead of searching for the missing and burying the dead. I understand both sides of the issue, but putting people at risk should be part of the equation. MAKE A DEAL!

What is the big deal about fixing the student loan rates? It should be no more than administrative cost and it should all be paid back by everyone. There should not be forgiveness for anyone or group of people, such as the congressional staff members. WHAT CONGRESS NEEDS TO INVESTIGATE IS THE DISPARITY IN COLLEGE TUITIONS.

QBAMASCARE, is scaring everyone. Originally Medi Care cost were never projected for what they are today or what they were projected to be back in the 60's. It was added on to help get the civil rights bill passed. Too many people are talking about the administration difficulty. The regulations are conflicting and the bill is being delivered piece meal and unlawfully. Hillary is not going to be happy if she has to defend this legislation during her run for the presidency, she has enough of her own problems.

Something is wrong when one in three Americans are on food stamps. If you can't review and solve this problem, then ask Michelle for help. I will be happy to pass along some ideas to her to get her started. It is obvious the people in charge of it now do not have the original intent of the program in mind. Maybe I'm wrong, but I doubt it. DO SOMETHING.

July 10, 2013

President Barack Obama

1600 Pennsylvania Avenue N.W.

Washington D.C. 20500

Dear President Obama,

The elephants are going to try some political posturing in an attempt to put off Obamascare, all phases, for another year. This will be costly, as there are, thousands of employees that have to be paid or furloughed. The other side of this, is if it takes two years to implement this law because it's complicated, maybe you should start over again, like I suggested. Maybe you can make a deal to save the part that will cover people with preexisting conditions. Something is better than nothing.

Tell Harry to get off this filibuster band wagon and work on some meaningful legislation. The man needs to retire and sit by the pool. He does not understand the spirit of consideration and compromise.

The more the donkeys complicate legislation, the less chances of it getting passed. If the poor and middle class ever wake up and realize what they are really doing to them, what will take place in this country, will make the Egyptian demonstrations look like a festival. Simple laws produce simple results when the government uses simple methods to implement and monitor them, SIMPLE.

Simple legislation, student loans, principle plus reasonable administration costs equals payment. Provide a list of schools that offer the best return on their investment and schools that cost more are their burden.

Simple legislation, secure the borders this year. Next year introduce employer mandates to verify employee status, no verification, send them to a verification center for investigation and a temporary work permit. Do not punish them unless they don't want to cooperate or they have a criminal background, if so, send them home.

Simple tax reform, no deductions and everyone pays a flat rate depending on their income, BUT EVERYONE PAYS.

July 11, 2013

President Barack Obama

1600 Pennsylvania Avenue N.W.

Washington D.C. 20500

Dear President Obama,

It's tough running a country that doesn't know who they are, isn't it? The country is being flooded with immigrants and they all think they own America. I can understand how they can be confused. We live in a country that does not have an official language or the guts to tell the people to drop the prefix to American. You the donkeys and the elephants want to keep it that way for your political advantages.

Pass a law that makes it illegal to describe yourself as a prefix American, in other words, make it illegal to be called Spanish, Black, Italian, Indian, Asian, African, or any other form of nationality except AMERICAN. We have eliminated words that certain groups don't like but still use, so why not the prefix to American.

The BALA organization is concerned about the influx of too many immigrants hurting their community in America. They are not worried about it hurting America. They should be more concerned about helping their community get ahead through education and family values versus keeping people out. I don't like their segregation, but I agree with their concern.

THE BORDERS NEED TO BE SHUT DOWN UNTIL WE AS A NATION RECOGONIZE WHO WE ARE, WHAT WE ARE, AND WHAT WE STAND FOR.

The congress needs to address these problems and give America a fixed identity. Once we know who we are, we can start solving our problems as a nation, not white, black, Hispanic, or any other color or group. This will not eliminate prejudice in our country, only honest family values will do that, but it will stop the fractionalization over time. This might bring the classes closer together and help eliminate our poor class.

Someone has to lead and the last time I looked that was your job. You have to put your political and personal persuasions aside and do what is right for AMERICA. Gut it out.

July 12, 2013

President Barack Obama

1600 Pennsylvania Avenue N.W.

Washington D.C. 20500

Dear President Obama,

It takes a lot of nerve to face the youth of America and stick it to them at the same time. You can bail out the banks, AIG, the unions and General Motors, and waste millions on green energy, but you can't do anything about the student loan program and Dog Track Harry. I guess making an estimated 51 billion isn't enough, you want more off the backs of the students. You are truly the flimflam man. You should be embarrassed to go to any college and speak.

Janet is gone, there is still a God out there. The down side is she is going to liberal California. I don't think she could do any more damage there then they have already done. Good bye, good reddens and I hope she will enjoy her fat paycheck.

I wonder if she is leaving because she twisted arms to get money for the Organization for Action, nothing more than the Federal Mafia, as far as I'm concerned. They are collecting money to promote legislation that is going to make the poor in this country poorer. I wouldn't donate one penny to any political organization and I will never understand why people donate. I still don't understand how you got reelected.

You are creating a media shield to protect reporters from the government or from the Obama Administration. Who is going to protect the people from all the laws your administration violates? Holder lied to congress and the American people and comes up with a lame excuse for doing it. Why do you have someone working for you that doesn't know what a paper trail can do to you? Why is he still working for you?

Have you ever noticed where the media hides the stories when it doesn't present you in a good image? I had to really search for the Janet and Holder stories. A good thing there is Fox News, the rest of the media on line buried the stories. They are not doing you any favors.

July 13, 2013

President Barack Obama

1600 Pennsylvania Avenue N.W.

Washington D.C. 20500

Dear President Obama,

I have never said thank you for reading my letters. I know the mail room reads the letters and responds and maybe one has slipped through to you, but I don't think that would be the case. I hope they put the different ideas the people submit in a report and pass them on. They have to be a lot better than what congress is coming up with. Regardless, thank you for accepting and responding to my letters whoever you are.

I hope you are enjoying the book I sent you. It is not flattering, but it is honest and my only agenda is helping America and Americans. I write how I feel and don't edit my letters to make them sound better. You read who I am at the moment, which most of the time is 5am in the morning.

The Zimmerman verdict is a victory for all Americans. We may not all agree, but I feel the jury made the right decision. The real problem we are not addressing is why we need a neighborhood watch in the first place. I believe that working people are tired people and don't have time to cause trouble like idle people. It would be great if all Americans were working, but that doesn't seem to be the main focus of you or the congress.

We are producing more gasoline on our own than we ever did, so why is the price of gas going up? The stock market is doing well, but why aren't more people working? The housing market is slowly improving, but why do we still have over seven million homes in foreclosure? We are spending billions on Obamascare and it hasn't started coverage yet? Too many questions and very few solutions and we have 435 congress people and 100 senators, you and your staff and nothing is getting better for the poor or the middle class. I see Hillary and Bill are doing well. Two hundred thousand to hear her speak about how she didn't do her job well.

I GUESS IT PAYS TO BE A POLITICAN. MAYBE WE SHOULD HAVE MEANS TESTING FOR ALL POLITICANS BEFORE THEY RECEIVE THEIR PENSIONS, OR WHAT DOES IT MATTER!

July 14, 2013

President Barack Obama

1600 Pennsylvania Avenue N.W.

Washington D.C. 20500

Dear President Obama,

The real tragedy in the memory of Trayvon Martin is the emphasis the people are putting on the fact Zimmerman was acquitted. The attention should turn to the American that are killed every day in our big cities. Three day before or after the Trayvon Martin shooting, in Florida, a police woman was shot three time in the face and died, by a black criminal. This was in Melbourne, Florida and no one demonstrated for her rights.

These demonstrations are a crock of crap. Trayvon Martin was an American boy killed by an American adult who was afraid for his life, during an altercation. The media, you and the NAACP have nothing better to do than incite people to riot and demonstrate. Justice was served and the man was found not guilty, end of story, like it ends in thousands of other murder cases. The difference here is you stuck your two cents where it doesn't belong because you wanted to make it political. You need to decide if you are an American? The whole population needs to make that same decision. It is time for the media, the government and the politicians to realize, they live in America, not black America, or Hispanic America, or white America, but America.

This fire has been burning for hundreds of years in this country and history can't be changed. Living a memory is not the answer to a strong America. Civil rights leaders that take advantage of their community should be exposed for what they really are, leaches on society. Where are they when children get gunned down in the streets of New York and Chicago? I don't see them calling for demonstrations or helping to root out the gangs that kill their brethren. It is all show and insensitive to all American victims.

Holder calling for an investigation into the Martin case is Jesse James becoming a banker. There were no civil rights violations. This is not a case of being sent to the back of the bus, but a case of two men fighting and they did what came natural for fear of dying, they killed the other person, just like men and women do in combat. The jury spoke, let it stand.

July 15, 2013

President Barack Obama

1600 Pennsylvania Avenue N.W.

Washington D.C. 20500

Dear President Obama,

I think in everyone's life they face some sort of prejudice by other people. It could be color, race, and sex, being fat, being poor, or being rich. Prejudice wares many faces, but the reality in the world today is it boils down to good people or bad people. Hate and ignorance are the drivers that prevent peaceful coexistence today. Stupidity is a close third, but what I think surpasses all obstacles are people's lack of reality to the situations they are in and the inner drive to change these situations. The government will never be able to do that for them no matter how much money they spend to correct it.

People and leaders use color, race and sex as an excuse for their failures and politicians and organizations use it as an excuse to raise money and maintain divisiveness. We all live under one flag, but we wave many different flags. This has been and will always be our shot coming to a united country. We stand together under threats and disasters, but we can't live together without fostering controversy among ourselves. Our good deeds seldom get rewarded, but our bad deeds are always noted and blown out of proportion.

Violence takes many lives in our country every day. Unarmed people are gunned down in the streets too often, so what makes the Martin case any different, nothing really except the media hype and coverage and comments by you and other black leaders. You fueled the fire of hatred over a common occurrence in this country just because you thought it was a white man, not a good or bad man. People and children of all race, color, and sex are being killed every day by people of all race, color and sex, so why does this case matter more than any other? It really doesn't, other than the fact that you as the president wouldn't stand up against the likes of Sharpton and other leaders that wanted to grab their 15 minutes of fame. You made it personal rather than presidential. PEOPLE THAT PUT YOU IN OFFICE LOOKED PAST YOUR COLOR AND AT A MAN THAT MADE PROMISES FOR A BETTER COUNTRY. You crossed the line Mr. President, you put your feeling before you put the unity of your country.

SHAME ON YOU.

July 16, 2013

President Barack Obama

1600 Pennsylvania Avenue N.W.

Washington D.C. 20500

Dear President Obama,

Dog Track Harry threatened the elephants and they caved. The feckless bunch made a deal for the Consumer Financial Bureau that will not be regulated by congress. So, why do we need congress if they are going to give their rights and power away? Now we are spending more money we don't have. ONE FOR THE DONKEYS AND DUNG FOR THE ELEPHANTS.

I AM SURPRIZED THE LABOR UNIONS ARE TALKING TO YOU AFTER THE DUMMIES FINALLY FIGURED OUT THEY ARE GOING TO GET THE SHORT END OF THE ROPE WITH OBAMASCARE. What kind of deal did you make with them for the labor board appointments? You must have promised them something.

Isn't congress wonderful? They are the most egotistical, clueless, bunch of misfits, we have running the country. They spend more than they make, they have no clue about how many agencies there are out there spending money, they don't punish their own for breaking the laws, they give you a pass every time you break the law, and they constantly screw the poor and middle class. You and they are a perfect match, the elephants trying to pin the tail on the donkey.

Holder needs to go. Who hasn't been stopped by the police in their lifetime? The Zimmerman case had nothing to do with the standup law and since it has been in place in Florida, the crime rate has dropped 23%. Where are the demonstrations for the people killed in Chicago? Could any of them look like your son? He is a hypocrite and you are his Godfather, perfect together.

The day is coming when this will all fall apart on you and the donkeys. The more you hurt people in the pocket, eventually they will turn on you and your legacy. Fortunately for you, the only thing they can hurt is your legacy, you can't be elected again, thank God. I wish I could praise you for your work, but it is impossible. You are more interested in being Barack Obama, then being, President Barack Obama.

July 17, 2013

President Barack Obama

1600 Pennsylvania Avenue N.W.

Washington D.C. 20500

Dear President Obama,

Every kid in America, at one point in their life, has been told, don't go where you don't belong, don't start trouble and don't talk to people you don't know. It is a crock of crap to think that this advice is only given to black or Hispanic children. I HEARD IT MORE THAN ONCE IN MY LIFETIME AND I STILL GIVE THAT ADVICE TO MY CHILDREN AND GRANDCHILDREN. There are people that make a living on hate mongering and some of them are your friends and frequent visitors at the Whitehouse. These people don't belong in the Whitehouse and neither do you, unless you want to start doing your job.

If people were working, they wouldn't be demonstrating. Instead of pushing Obamascare, maybe you should concentrate on jobs and how to create them without increasing the size of government. Did you ever work for anyone or run a business or were you always on the government payroll, what did they call it, an organizer. This sounds like the navigators you want Obamascare to hire to push the program. In real life they are called sales people and they are paid on their results, not hype.

The next time you talk to Holder, tell him this man will be glad to talk to him about race relations. The only COWARD I see is him because he can't tell people the truth and accept the responsibility for his actions. It is a travesty what black people and leadership do to other black people and you and the government do nothing about it. Stop blaming it on the rest of the world and the people that are trying to help them. You can start with that defunct department of education and work your way down to family values.

The truth of the matter is there will always be prejudice in the world, it is natural. People have hated other people and countries since the beginning of time. The only equalizer is money. The fact is rich people don't hang with poor people, they hang with other rich white, black Hispanic or even green people. Success hides prejudice better than failure because they are on the same level. It is just a fact of life that people have a hard time understanding. Success doesn't recognize color, only accomplishment.

July 18, 2013

President Barack Obama

1600 Pennsylvania Avenue N.W.

Washington D.C. 20500

Dear President Obama,

You are starting to sound like the donkey's ass. You don't have a clue and neither does anyone else, for that matter, what the real cost of Obamascare will cost the people. They didn't have a clue when they passed Medicare either and look where it is today. It was an add on to the civil rights bill. Stop wasting time and money telling Americans how good it is, it isn't. Pass a simple law that states, all people are required to have health insurance and all insurance companies have to cover them. There is a way to do it and it shouldn't be a government problem. The exception would be Medicare.

The verdict in the Zimmerman case should be respected. The jury gave up their personal life for weeks and came to a conclusion. Why have a jury system if you are going to measure every decision they make. It's history and belongs in the library.

Why did everyone involved in the Benghazi incident have to sign nondisclosure statements? Is this another Holder cover up? Where is the transparency you promised?

The congress and the senate need a mandatory retirement age as well as the Supreme Court. It is time for the dog track crowd to move on and give other people a chance to collect the benefits. Maybe a younger group will be more productive and reform some of the antiquated laws we don't enforce.

The editor from Rolling Stone needs a boulder dropped on his head to knock some sense into it. He should be charged with stupidity and sent into time out.

Why do we allow teenagers to quit school? Graduating high school should not be optional. Why does the department of education support states that have teachers who can't pass minimal skills examines?

Again, anytime you and the coward, Holder, want to have a realistic discussion on how to help the poor and minority groups, call me. I will be happy to tell you like it is and how to fix it. Of course, a more educated society might not bode well for the donkey party, so there is some risk involved on your part.

July 19, 2013

President Barack Obama

1600 Pennsylvania Avenue N.W.

Washington D.C. 20500

Dear President Obama,

Thirty five years ago, could you walk the streets of Chicago and be safer than people are today? What are you doing about black on black crime, for that matter, what are you doing about the high crime rates in the big cities? You are a hypocrite. Maybe we need special legislation to control the gangs and clubs that have criminal agendas. Don't worry about their rights, you and Holder have crapped on the Constitution enough, a little more won't hurt.

You need to stop the states from given children the right to quit school. If the children have attitudes about learning, then set up boot camp schools that will educate and provide alternatives to quitting. Once you have quit school, you quit living. It is time to bring back the truant officers and weed the attitudes out and put them in a tuff environment until they realize that being tuff doesn't pay, being smart does.

This hype about the stand your ground laws is a bunch of crap. Most people didn't even know it existed until Holder made a big deal out of it. The stand your ground law had nothing to do with the Martin case. People are getting tired of being pushed around? Do you think any person that fights back is doing it because they want the protection of the stand your ground law, what part of that don't you understand? They can't depend on government for protection, so they take matters into their own hands. They fear for their life, not the law.

Why don't you stand up for America instead of propelling the race, gender, and class differences in our society? You, the donkeys and the elephants helped perpetuate this problem by injecting it into your campaigns for elections, so you are as guilty as the person that commits a civil rights violation.

I started writing these letters because I wanted to help you and our country, but you have been blinded by your own ego and your loyalty to a jackass. Like you have given up on the children and the victims in our country, I will not quit writing these letters. I hope you read the book I sent you because another is on the way. The next time you shoot hoops, think about all the kids, LIKE YOU, that will never get a chance to take a shot because they were SHOT.

July 20, 2013

President Barack Obama

1600 Pennsylvania Avenue N.W.

Washington D.C. 20500

Dear President Obama,

I suggest that you delay the entire Obamascare program for a year and for you to personally get involved in the restructure of the program. I agree with you that everyone should have health insurance, but that is not what everyone wants. The healthy, young generation doesn't want to spend their money on insurance and doesn't understand the value of it for later years. The industry will survive and cost less if everyone was on a plan.

This is my solution to the problem. Congress should pass a law that states insurance companies have to cover all people with universal coverage in every state. This will cover the people in every state even if they move or travel. People should not have to change coverage every time they move or change careers. The insurance companies will come up with a solution to the problem with government support. Leave everything status quo until they come up with the solution. This is not a government problem and people will have to understand to get quality care at minimum costs requires that everyone be covered.

Think of it this way, insurance companies insuring a person from the day they are born till the day they die, no changes of coverage or company. We are covered by health insurance in our auto policy, our workers compensation policy, sports policies, and our regular health care and these paper companies are all making a profit. More profit is being made by the paper pushers than the medical providers.

This would require that you have a strong and enforceable immigration policy in place and that is a government problem. Concentrate on that while the insurance companies concentrate on full coverage for everyone.

I am still available to talk to you and Holder about race relations any time you want. The only way to help people is to support them in wanting to help themselves. We learn our prejudices from family, life experiences and our failure to understand our limitations.

July 21, 2013

President Barack Obama

1600 Pennsylvania Avenue N.W.

Washington D.C. 20500

Dear President Obama,

On the road again to tell people what you are going to do about the economy, that a crock! Save the gas and expense of traveling and show me the results, not the rhetoric. You are way pass the days of wining and dining and you need to fix Obamascare before that tanks the economy more. You have Obamascare, immigration, student loans, Benghazi, the IRS, and that despicable and dysfunctional staff that need your attention. Stop making speeches and start doing something worthwhile.

The donkeys and elephants are working on major tax reform and getting advice and pressure from corporation like GE and Microsoft, what's up with that? Are you going to let them write the bill like the fed did? Tell congress to close the doors, put their brains before their mouth, review the laws and make common sense decisions, if they can't do that, tell them to quit. Do not get your staff involved or that will really mess things up since we know they are inches away from GE's butt.

Boehner needs to go. It is his job to collect ideas and guide congress to come up with laws that make common sense. It would be simple for him to pass one segment of the law at a time. Once you see positive results from border security, move on to the next segment of immigration that makes sense. We have eleven million people here that have to be accounted for and the stupid logic of they broke the law. They are here trying to survive and in most cases providing a service and doing a good job. We break the law by providing them jobs, so who is the law breaker. Register them, separate the good from the bad, send the bad back and set a path for the good to become citizens. If they are only here for the money, send them back also. The jackasses and elephants that are complaining about amnesty, are the same people that allow them to work in their states.

THE BOTTOM LINE IS, STAY HOME, START GIVING DIRECTION, FOLLOW UP, AND MONITOR THE PROGRESS AND RESULTS. STOP BEING THE FLIMFLAM MAN.

July 22, 2013

President Barack Obama

1600 Pennsylvania Avenue N.W.

Washington D.C. 20500

Dear President Obama,

You are meeting with your supporters and it is always good to get the pats on the back, but it is smarter to know what your adversaries are doing and thinking. They may have some ideas that are similar or better and knowing how you want to do what is right for America, maybe you could latch on to those ideas and move them along. I would check you back after your supporters leave. They don't have your best interest in mind and they are controlled by a jackass, not the best qualifier for intelligent decisions and ideas.

Why are the banks and brokerage houses stock piling commodities? This is been going on for months and the SEC is finally getting around to investigating it. This is just a massive effort to stick it to the poor and middle class and they are way ahead of you. Who can you trust and who is getting the benefit of this?

I am still ready to have a talk with Holder and you about race relations of all Americans. We can also discuss immigration, gun control, and fiscal management. Of course, we cannot leave out transparency in your administration. Have you discussed the merit of children not being able to quit school until they graduate or have a marketable skill?

I really think you and congress have to have a serious discussion about gangs and clubs in this country that have survived on criminal activities. This might be a violation of their civil rights, but I think the framers of the Constitution didn't have criminal activities in mind that are contrary to the moral values in America. When kids think they can't make it in society, they take the low road and that is costly in blood and money.

Delay all of Obamascare for a year and put out a better program. This is really an industry problem, not a government problem. Let this common sense move bring the people on your side and garner more support. A stronger program will give it a better chance of survival. THE QUESTION IS ARE YOU STRONG ENOUGH TO DO IT?

July 23, 2013

President Barack Obama

1600 Pennsylvania Avenue N.W.

Washington D.C. 20500

Dear President Obama,

Sommers to replace Bernanke, are you kidding me? The government has no control over the fed and you want this loose cannon running it. A person of Christine Lagarde's caliber would be a better choice. You can't keep bringing in people that put America on the edge in the past. The simple qualification is someone who believes we shouldn't spend more than we take in. That would be tough right now, but as a nation we can get there if we work together. Pursue due diligence in this matter, not cronyism.

This tour you are taking on the tax payers dime is nothing more than to conjure up support for the democrats that are running in November. You have done nothing to help the economy or create jobs. Your major contribution is threating companies with Obamascare causing them to put off any commitments to growth. The market is being driven by profits and greed and costing the American people big time. Stay home and start doing your job. The donkey party is not paying you, the American people are!

ACCORDING TO THE POLLS THE COUNTRY IS LOOSING FAITH IN YOU AND THE CONGRESS, WHAT PART OF THIS DON'T YOU UNDERSTAND. YOU ARE GOING TO GO OFF ON THE RICH VERSUS THE POOR AGENDA AND YOU ARE THE CAUSE AND PART OF THE PROBLEM. YOU AND THE DONKEYS SHOULD CALL YOURSELF THE ENTITLEMENT PARTY.

You have a major problem with the banks and brokerage houses buying and storing commodities, so what are you going to do about it? I know, stand in line and wait for your share of the political contributions. Remove the tax deductions from political contributions and see how much money you will get. Every dollar donated by a company is costing the poor people, they have to get it from somewhere. My Father told me 60 years ago, the government can't give you something they don't take from you somewhere else. You have gone beyond the else and are taking it from all the poor people around the world. You are the problem, not the solution!

July 24, 2013

President Barack Obama

1600 Pennsylvania Avenue N.W.

Washington D.C. 20500

Dear President Obama,

Step up to the plate, the student loan program should be a cost effective program, not a profit enterprise. It shouldn't be any more than 1% interest plus justifiable administrative cost. The loan should only apply to approved colleges and occupational schools for functional majors, in other words, not basket weaving.

Janet Yellen should be your choice to run the fed. Summers was partially responsible for the 2008 financial mess. I don't know much about Janet Yellen, but I will take a qualified woman over a man because of their organizational skills, any day.

You need to understand this and all the supporters of the Trayvon Martin tragedy, YOU DON'T NEED TO BE BLACK TO KNOW WHAT IT FEELS LIKE TO WALK IN TRAVON MARTIN'S SHOES. Did you ever know a white person that lived in a black neighborhood?

Caroline Kennedy would be a great choice for Ambassador to Japan, just make sure she is properly protected. There are no safe places in a transit world.

Congress has already screwed up the SNAP program, have Michelle work with the food manufactures and code the products that are essential for good health and nutrition. Special pricing should also be a consideration in her efforts. If Michelle doesn't want to get involved, I understand, working with the government is not a pleasant experience. I am sure you know that.

Education, allowing children to quit school is dumb and a major cause of crime and deprivation in this country. Children with special behavioral needs should be evaluated and educated so they fit into society. Allowing them to quit is not the answer and allowing them to sit and learn nothing is the answer. Special schools away from their environment should be established to make them successful. Mr. Martins statistics are shocking, 52% of black males and 58% of Hispanic males don't graduate high school. This is a catastrophic failure of the department of education that receives seventy seven billion dollars.

I am still available to discuss, with you and Holder, the merits of race relations in our country. Give me a call.

July 25, 2013

President Barack Obama

1600 Pennsylvania Avenue N.W.

Washington D.C. 20500

Dear President Obama,

You are going to allow the IRS to spend 700 million dollars advertising Obamascare? The IRS can't figure out or be ready to launch the entire program and they are spending this money on a crap shoot. YOU WILL NEED THIS 700 MILLION DOLLARS TO PAY FOR THE SUBSIDIES YOU ARE GOING TO ALLOW WITHOUT VERIFICATION. HOW DUMB IS THIS.

Are you aware that the government contracts out Medicare to private insurance companies because they can't handle the program? If HHS can't handle Medicare, why are you giving it to a department that has a worse track record then them? I like the fact that you want to give everyone full coverage, but you have to delay the program, fix it and do it right.

NSA spying, is this a joke? There is no privacy in people's lives. What is the big deal about listening to phone calls? You have Facebook, Twitter, credit cards, phones, black boxes in cars, bank records and now medical records and they can all tell the authorities where you are, what you're doing and where you have been. WHAT IS THE BIG SECRET?

I SUGGESTED A FEW LETTERS AGO, Yellen over Summers, it is a no brainer. New blood, fresh ideas and maybe less connections to the Wall Street crowd.

Why are you wasting time on voter rights? Texas has a right to regulate voting. The solution is simple, identification please. The problem is complicated by the fact that this is a political agenda and not a voting rights agenda. This is the donkeys trying to override state authority to keep their voting edge, especially in the entitlement crowd. You are playing the race card here again.

When the Koran states very clearly and the Muslin leadership supports, THOU SHALL NOT KILL, then you can have them at my house for dinner, until then, take them to a diner and pay for it yourself. I do not see or hear daily condemnation of their quest for world domination and their support of women's rights.

JUST SO YOU KNOW, PHONY SCANDALS DON'T PRODUCE DEAD VICITIMS!

July 26, 2013

President Barack Obama
1600 Pennsylvania Avenue N.W.
Washington D.C. 20500

Dear President Obama,

You are like a kid with an attitude, your frustration with congress is your own doing. You are dealing with a bunch of brats with huge egos. If you want to get the edge on congress, call me and I will tell you what to do. I write these letters and it helps with my frustration and I hope you will wake up some day and see you and your legacy are being used by the donkeys. All these different views that congress has mean nothing. You are the leader of the nation, good or bad, but if you believe you're right then take measures and lead.

The CMS is restricting new and some old providers from going on Obamascare. This is a good thing. What's bad, there is still major waste and fraud in the system and that must be stopped or Obamascare will never succeed. They need to put checks and balance in place to stop the fraud and waste and use the people to do it. The solution and the monitoring is simple and the problem will take care of itself. You need to think out of the box. I'll send you a ladder if you need one.

Stop taking credit for creating jobs. The only thing you have done is make government bigger and sluggish. I told you to start a Nation Disaster Response Team that would create some jobs, important and needed jobs. Make a deal with Keystone that would create jobs.

I have a solution for your e verify program and immigration reform. It would be an employer based solution that would supplement immigration verification.

Larry Summers is not the right man for the job, old guard and old school. Select Yellen and start cracking the gridlock with congress.

Did you ever consider how this country was built and the initial guidance was a couple pieces of paper called the Constitution. Now we have mega laws and mega problems and we are going backwards, that is a fact.

BRING HOME THE TROOPS AND STOP SUPPORTING COUNTRIES THAT ARE KILLING THERE OWN PEOPLE.

July 27, 2013

President Barack Obama

1600 Pennsylvania Avenue N.W.

Washington D.C. 20500

Dear President Obama,

Mr. President, is the light on at home? Where did you get your bogus figures for the pipeline? You need inspectors for the pipeline, they have pumping stations that must be monitored and maintained, they will need repair crews and maintenance crews and they will have to paint the exposed surfaces. Make a deal for low gas prices or charge them for product flow to offset gas prices. Think out of the box. Technology will develop a way to reduce carbon emissions. You can create some jobs with the stroke of the pen, DO IT!

There is an income gap because there is an intelligence gap. There is an income gap because people quit school and give up on life. The government is a perfect example of this. Low intelligence, high income and poor results. Why are we bringing people in from other countries to fill jobs? We have an intelligence gap. Wake up in Washington, you are the problem.

You want to do something intelligent, INCREASE THE TAX ON PAPER PUSHERS FOR PROFIT AND DECREASE THE TAX ON MANUFACTURING AND SERVICE PROVIDERS.

NBC is going to do a miniseries on Hillary. Is GE using their media company to elect the next President? Isn't she afraid she will be over exposed to radiation? Are they going to do this for all the candidates? A miniseries on how to kill four Americans and get away with it. Where is the no justice no peace crowd?

Please advise Rand Paul that we gave all our freedoms away when the people started getting entitlements. It influences our vote, diminishes our spirits and makes us reliant on a dysfunctional government, not to mention the donkeys and elephants that take full advantage of the situation.

The CEO of Siemens is losing his job because of lack of performance and results. The good part is they don't have to wait four years to force him out. Just a thought!

July 28, 2013

President Barack Obama
1600 Pennsylvania Avenue N.W.
Washington D.C. 20500

Dear President Obama,

Lunch with Hillary, how nice, are you going to discuss Benghazi, the middle east talks, the fact that you continue to supply weapons there in the name of promoting democracy, or will you decide how much to give the Palestinians to stay quiet for a while? Maybe you will discuss a Hillary and Michelle ticket?

Meanwhile, the country suffers from poor job growth, Obamascare deficiencies and mysteries, more gun violence, massive waste and fraud in the government, and more doctors dropping Medicare, just to name a few problems. Enjoy your lunch.

When people can't find jobs they look for alternative income sources, such as, SS Disability, food stamps, extended unemployment, and welfare, when in fact none of this would be needed if they could go to work and earn a decent income. I wonder what a store would look like if you had a section for American made products and a section for foreign made products. I don't think I would like the results. It would be a clear indicator of how many jobs we lost over the years. Give it some thought!

Will Holder go after the states that legalize marijuana, a violation of federal law, the same way he is going after states on voting rights. What are we going to do about second hand smoke, no marijuana sections? Is this going to be a domestic product or imported. I wonder how many people will die in the process of supplying marijuana. Is marijuana an approved drug in Obamascare?

I suggest you do a sweep of all congressional and senate offices and remove the alcoholic beverages, marijuana, and other drugs of choice. Keep a list and use it when you need an extra vote here and there. You never know, this may be what is causing gridlock. Just a thought!

July 29, 2013

President Barack Obama

1600 Pennsylvania Avenue N.W.

Washington D.C. 20500

Dear President Obama,

I know you are worried about grid lock in the congress, but you are not handling it the right way. Meeting with each group separately is counterproductive. Meet with them every week together and defuse their egos and their affiliations to the donkeys and the elephants. You need to speak for America and so do them. You need deal with the obstacles and start applying common sense solutions, not like Obamascare, over regulated and confusing.

The congressional session is too short. Working 126 days in session is an insult to every hard working person. Going home to listen to the people is a load of dung. They have a staff that will answer letters and phone calls and consolidate it in a report. They pass less than 10% of the bills that are presented and that is a dismal performance. Maybe it is time for you to get in their face while they are together. You need to do what is right for America and you are not.

Holder's law suits regarding the voting rights act are a waste of time. Simple requirements, American citizen and the ability to read write and speak English. If you can't read or write how can you make a decision based on the information that is available? If you can't speak English, how can you understand the conversation and debates the candidates have? If you are relying on another person's interpretation, is that your vote or their vote? If the federal government wants to get involved, have them put a representative at every voting place on Election Day to mediate disputes rather then you looking for law suits.

Congress people and senators that are not present to vote while in session should be replaced by the state's governor. American deserve at least that for the money and benefits they pay for representation. Congress should work a full schedule like the rest of America.

This is a real joke, a hundred elephant donors have signed a letter prompting the elephants in office to get on with it and pass immigration reform. When should they do this, congress is off for a month. Shouldn't they pass immigration reform because it is the right thing to do or do we need to wait for these donors to instruct congress? If this is the case Mr. President, why aren't you following the suggestions I send you every day? How did your lunch date go?

July 30, 2013

President Barack Obama

1600 Pennsylvania Avenue N.W.

Washington D.C. 20500

Dear President Obama,

Tell the donkeys to stop wasting their time on racial profiling, it isn't the color of a person skin that police are concerned with, but the behavior of people that may be in the wrong place. People that are in jail are not there because of the color of their skin, they did something wrong. The core problem is why there is a distortional amount of blacks and Hispanics in jail. The answer is simple, and solution are simple, the government allowed them to become quitters early in life. Education breeds confidence and confidence breeds success and they never had a fair shot at either. I am still available to talk about race relation with you and Holder, just call.

Thirty seven million dollars paid to dead farmers. We need tax reform, but you will never solve that problem until you stop waste, fraud and mismanagement in government. The government continues to borrow money because of their lousy performance and stupid business decisions. This is at every level and in every department. The government has set lazy standards for work and results. A good look at the congressional work schedule indicates that. You will never have fair tax reform until you can substantiate how much it cost to operate the government effectively. YOU MUST STOP THROWING GOOD MONEY ON BAD MONEY.

It is a fair statement to say that the black community expected more from you when you were elected President. The truth is the entire population expected more of you when you were elected. You have done more to hurt all the people in this country because of your loyalty to the donkeys. You will never the poor in this country by giving them money and entitlements. This is the typical policy of the donkeys to keep people dependent on them so they can secure their vote. The elephants are just as bad because they are part of the problem. It is a constant battle over money but never over results. Neither party wants to solve the real problem, for the donkeys, its more money, for the elephants, its less money and no solutions.

It is time for you and the politicians to look at the root of problems and stop blaming them on the racial and class divide in this country. It is time to understand that all people are not created equal but should be treated equal. It is time to understand that environments have to change along with education to make people successful and that leads to equality. It is time to be AMERICANS.

July 31, 2013

President Barack Obama
1600 Pennsylvania Avenue N.W.
Washington D.C. 20500

Dear President Obama,

You gave the boys in the band a pep talk so they can support Obamascare, which is an illusion, a new immigration bill to replace the current one we can't enforce effectively, and jobs for the middle class when you should address the problems from the bottom up. Is everybody happy? By the time they get back from their summer vacation they will have forgotten everything you said. Good move, motivation before vacation.

Stop stating that the pipeline will only create 50 jobs, your handlers are making you look like the democratic mascot. This is the problem with you and the government, you don't understand that everything starts with one, coke built a world market selling one bottle of coke at a time, and many major corporations started with one employee. Because you don't understand that one penny is as important as one million dollars, you waste millions of dollars and shrug it off like the people that throw pennies away in the parking lot and I still pick them up when I see them. I also waste money, but not on the same scale the government does.

Imagine this, you take one poor person that quit school, you educate them in a marketable skill and encourage responsibility and let them experience success. This one person doesn't have to be stopped by police, doesn't have to be arrested, doesn't have to clog up the courts, doesn't have to go to jail, doesn't have to go on welfare and doesn't have to be dependent on the government for the rest of their life. The down side is, this one person may never vote democratic again and the donkeys lose a voter. It sounded good till the last part when it had a direct effect on you hypocrites. You're scared because SUCCESS CAN BE CONTAGIOUS.

Why would laws need racial impact statements if the government was doing everything they could to make its people productive and successful at all levels? Who monitors the success of the government? How can government be successful when two parties are always manipulating the people against each other? What authority holds politicians to their promises and punishes them for their lies and crimes on the same par with the people? Somewhere in this calamity a leader must emerge, so where is he or she or it?

August 1, 2013

President Barack Obama

1600 Pennsylvania Avenue N.W.

Washington D.C. 20500

Dear President Obama,

John Koskinen is a good appointment for the IRS, a department that is long overdue for restructure. The tax code they enforce also needs a major overhaul. The disparity in our tax laws is one reason so many people cheat on their taxes. Another reason is Americans don't like seeing their taxes wasted intentionally or inadvertently. Every individual should contribute to the general fund. Refunding money is proof of the government's poor fiscal management. Unfortunately, reform and restructure can only be successful to a point, spending must be an important part of the equation. Deficits are not a good indicator of good legislation and fiscal management. We cannot continue to borrow money from the world piggy bank and write IOU's to entitlement funds.

The conservative Tea Party is a thorn in your side and rightfully so. Your lack of business management skills prompts you to make silly statements like the pipeline will only create 50 permanent jobs. They are a good check and balance and strong enough to keep the donkeys and elephants in line or sway them to better solutions. If everything was functioning right they would have never been elected. Compromise is good, but doing what is right and productive is better.

Jason Furman, are you kidding me? He helped engineer the stimulus package and formulate Obamascare and neither one has produce anything but controversy and confusion. What jobs did he help create? I hope he isn't the gem that provided the job count for the pipeline. You need a group of forensic accountants to give you advice and root out fiscal mismanagement before the checks go out. Every department pads their budget and is reckless with spending it, especially the congress and the senate. Find a better candidate.

You need to start telling the Americans the truth about future retirement. I hear the warnings and read it in the media, but I think Americans are too busy buying IPhones and IPads and don't truly understand the message. I applaud you in your efforts to help protect their investments, but I think Wall Street is shifting an unfair amount in their pockets. Commissions, bonuses and tax loopholes drive Wall Street's bottom line, not individuals secure finances. The people's money should be protected 100 %, let Wall Street gamble with their own profits and get them the hell out of the commodity business.

August 2, 2013

President Barack Obama

1600 Pennsylvania Avenue N.W.

Washington D.C. 20500

Dear President Obama,

Did congress exempt themselves from Obamascare before they left for vacation? I think they did but you do not see it on the front page. How is the plan supposed to succeed if companies and political groups are granted waivers? When the young people in this country wake up and find out how the donkeys and you are dealing them over financially, hell will break loose in this country. If they come off the pot long enough to wake up you will see a massive effort to self-destruct Obamascare. It won't take much for that to happen since it is in a self-destruction mode on its own. Some piece of signature legislation.

Maybe if you spent more time in Washington instead of campaigning all over the country, the immigration bill wouldn't be teetering on the border. I don't want to tell you about the number ONE again, but you didn't get it the first time. If you must do a complete bill in immigration, then have consecutive triggers in it as the law achieves positive results. It is an embarrassment to our country and the Department of Education, something like that, to be haggling over tech visas. Do we really need the technical help from other countries to get the job done in America? SECURE THE BORDER AND USE THE E VERIFY SYSTEM TO TRIGGER DOCUMENTATION AND A PATH TO CITIZENSHIP. ONE STEP AT A TIME, ONE.

The SNAP program, food stamps, has gone from 38 billion dollars to 78 billion dollars and we still have starving children in this country. Do you think something is wrong with that program? We give away free phone, SNAP is ready to break, social security paying dead people, department of agriculture paying 37 million to dead farmers, over 500 million lost on green energy projects, billions in Medicare fraud and waste and a dysfunctional IRS and they are in charge of Obamascare? What chance do you think Obamascare has of surviving? The point is this, FIX SOMETHING AND MAKE IT FUNCTION CORRECTLY.

I read a report that the government waste a half a trillion dollars a year. I found that hard to believe but now I think it is more than that. I don't know if you drink coffee, but you need something to wake you up.

August 3, 2013

President Barack Obama
1600 Pennsylvania Avenue N.W.
Washington D.C. 20500

Dear President Obama,

Happy Birthday, and many wishes for fond memories for you and your family on this day, I hope you score a 59 on your golf outing.

Your move to veto the ban by the ITC was justified. Patent infringements belong in the courts, not in the market place. Business is business. The free cell phone program has to stop. If it is true that the Mexican billionaire is making 470 million off this program that is a slap in the face of every taxpayer. I wish you could have the phone manufactures and the auto companies insert a device that will prevent texting and hand held phone conversations while driving. It would save a lot of innocent lives. I would rather spend 2.1 billion dollars on that rather than giving away free phone. Please do it and save a life.

The Asbury Park Press, an editorial supporter, did an article and video on my letters to you every day. You can see it on francismdelvecchio.com and I hope you do.

Back to business, the sequester is costing Americans financially, but I question if the government is getting real production and value from the contractors who do the work. I don't see the degree of pride and loyalty that once existed. It is all about money and benefits and that has put major cities and soon this country in financial peril. I think too much emphasis is put on a person life style and not their work ethic. This is a primary, but not the only, cause of waste and fraud in the government today. The government needs better negotiators formulating contracts with employees and contractors or better directions.

I will keep this short today, but I want you to know that I am still available to talk race relations with you and Holder any day.

August 4, 2013

President Barack Obama

1600 Pennsylvania Avenue N.W.

Washington D.C. 20500

Dear President Obama,

Tell the congress that cutting spending is the second part of the equation, stop waste, fraud, mismanagement and paying the DEAD. The problem requires austere fiscal management at every level of government. Naturally the donkey is on the wrong end of the cart again.

Waste, a good example is the voting rights law suits by the justice department. The solution is simple, you show valid ID like we have to do when we get on a plane. If you continue and lose the lawsuit, all the dead people that vote in Chicago won't be able to vote anymore. This is all about keeping the donkeys from losing votes in the different states and not about a person's right to vote. The voting is done at the state level and should be a state problem. I did not see you go after the people that were intimidating voters at the polling places with verbal and physical threats. Holder is pissing all over states' rights and picking and choosing what he likes from the Supreme Court. Fire the man for not acting like one. Have him look into why we are paying dead people and who is responsible. Why is Lois Lerner still getting a paycheck?

The federal government can't function normally itself, where do they get the gall to question the states? Obamascare is heading for a high speed derailment and a massive amount of wasted money. The elephants want to use the budget crisis as a tool to stop Obamascare and that is wrong. Pushing dung around is not the answer. Mr. President, step forward and delay Obamascare until you can fix it or it will plague you as a major failure in your administration. I would rather see a good functional program that will help people rather than the chaos this will cause. The program has some major benefits, but also, too many serious flaws. Stop it and fix it.

Smart move protecting the embassies. The truth of the matter is, if we have to protect them with armed force, then maybe we shouldn't be there. Where does this hate for our country come from? Are we minding other people's business too much for the sake of the dollar? This world will never unite until we are threatened by another universe and then there will be countries lined up to make a deal with them. You have enough to worry about in America!

August 5, 2013

President Barack Obama
1600 Pennsylvania Avenue N.W.
Washington D.C. 20500

Dear President Obama,

I hope you do a better job over hauling the mortgage problem than you did with Obamascare. I saw a comment about special conditions for low income families. Try this on for size, build a nice home that will fit the people's budget, not provide money they can't afford to borrow. Since you are still thinking of backing up these loans, collect the interest and leave the banks to loan their own money, not money protected by the government. The interest would be a good source of income. The homes in the community should be controlled by the community and standards for maintenance should be established just like senior communities. If necessary, use federal land to keep he prices down and give the home buyer the most for their money.

I have a great idea, since the chair of the appropriations committee, Barbara Milkulski, thinks she will be the catalyst for an agreement, let's have only one senator and three congress people from each state. That will reduce government by 319 congressmen and 50 senators. That would save a big chunk of money. Less people, better ideas, more efficient government and the results, better overall. You can start by getting rid of Dog Track Harry and Bullhead Boehner. You can have them produce simple law with simple solutions. Yeah, I know, I'm pipe dreaming.

The elephants are going to try and stop Obamascare so why don't you delay the process, like I told you a long time ago, and fix the problems. The IRS is not ready to deal with Obamascare. Give a good idea a chance to work. This is an insurance company problem and not a government. Tell the insurance companies, these are the rules, come up with a plan to move forward.

Did Holder get caught with his hand in the cookie jar? You never listen, I told you to get rid of him after the news incident. A four million dollar travel bill, does he take a plane to work? And the hits keep coming and you keep dodging the issues!

By the way, I will be on Fox News tomorrow to discuss my letters to you.

August 6, 2013

President Barack Obama

1600 Pennsylvania Avenue N.W.

Washington D.C. 20500

Dear President Obama,

When are you going to stop running around the country blaming the elephants for the gridlock in Washington. You are just as responsible. Leadership is the ability to bring opposing sides together and accomplish something, did you miss that in your Harvard Education? Get off the band wagon and start doing what has to be done.

It doesn't matter how low cost a mortgage is, if people can't afford it what's the sense. Build green energy homes that is modern, community controlled and affordable for the income a family earns. Stop trying to make the money the victim and pressuring banks to make loans. You are on the wrong end of the equation. If the government is going to insure the loan then they should retain the interest to offset the guarantee. Think out of the box.

"EDUCATION IS THE MOST POWERFUL WEAPON YOU CAN USE TO CHANGE THE WORLD" NELSON MANDELA, AMEN. The sequel to that is use that education to develop peace and prosperity throughout the world. I believe you are really afraid of helping the poor and immigrants in this country. You could lose control over a majority of your votes and that is why you and others use class and race as a weapon. When people figure out that we are all Americans, it will place the donkeys and elephants on notice, rightfully so.

Delay Obamascare and fix the problems. It is an insurance industry problem and not a government problem. Don't let a great idea fail because of stubbornness and egotism. Obamascare can survive and be a benefit to all Americans if you give it a chance. Garbage in is garbage out and that is what you have now.

To all the donkeys and elephants that want to stop a path to citizenship for the illegal immigrants, simple, they should have been stopped at the border, but since they are here deal with it in a humane and productive way. There are simple solutions to this problem, just think pass your emotions. Mr. President, concentrate more on your leadership and less on your speeches. We all know you can talk a good game.

August 7, 2013

President Barack Obama,

1600 Pennsylvania Avenue N.W.

Washington D.C. 20500

Dear President Obama,

Why did you cancel the summit meeting with Putin? This was your chance to stare him down, back him in the corner and show some guts. Who cares if they keep him there, maybe someday he will rat on them, maybe not, they have a different justice system over there. We protect the criminals and bury the victims, they just bury everybody involved, simple.

When you speak at the March on Washington are you going to tell them the truth? You couldn't do anything about gas, food and energy prices, but we will give you subsidies to help pay for health insurance so they can treat your starvation, depression and illnesses caused by lack of jobs but marijuana is on the way so you will feel better. Are you going to tell them we are considering special visas for foreigner students and workers because public education is dysfunctional in many towns across the country and that is why their children can't find suitable work. Are you going to suggest that it is the rich people that are causing these problems and not the waste and fraud that is rampant in the federal government? Are you going to tell them that the memo instructing transparency in your administration was shredded by mistake? I could go on but try a novel approach and tell the truth.

Congress has taken care of themselves again. They manipulated a way around Obamascare and the government is going to contribute toward that, how nice!

Mr. President, there are people all around the world that hate America, just do what you have to do to protect the country. I suggest you stop supplying weapons to the enemy that would help. You have supplied the Middle East with money we don't have, weapons and troops, all in the name of peace, I wonder! You need to reevaluate your decision process for the Middle East. I know it is a difficult situation.

You are a Harvard graduate, our public school teachers are college graduates, most doing a great job, they are directed by administrators that are college graduates, so how is all this intellectual power producing a high percentage of failure in our public schools? The poor and middle class suffer the most. Quitting school should never be an option for anyone. "Education is the most powerful weapon you can use to change the world." I suggest you research the person who stated that. Maybe we should supply less weapons and more books, good idea!

August 8, 2013

President Barack Obama

1600 Pennsylvania Avenue N.W.

Washington D.C. 20500

Dear President Obama,

I think you have greater problems than worrying about SOPA legislation, to prevent streaming on the internet. If the people cannot protect their own property, then that is their problem.

Why is the NSA using contractors it has very little control over to support their system? Reducing the contractors is not enough, eliminate them or hire them as employees so you have more control over them. You need to go to the NSA and kick some serious butt and find a new administrator, your man is not the man for the job.

Private e mail security companies are closing down because of government threats. Why don't you just hack into them like you do everything else? If it is too difficult to hack them, hire them to protect government information that the government can't protect on its own. This sounds like a violation of the first amendment rights to me. I wonder how many government officials use these services.

The Washington Power Plant is a major contributor to greenhouse gas emissions, what a surprise. This is like the shoemaker that doesn't have time to fix his own shoes. If the problem wasn't so serious, it would become the best joke in town. We wasted a half a billion dollars on Solyndra, but we are gassing congress and the senate, no wonder you people can't think straight, you all in a smog. So much for clean air, dumb!

Printing a manual on how to hide intelligence and deceive the public, is this a side effect of the emissions from the power plant? Why don't you mail a copy to al Qaida? Your administration continues to surface the waste, fraud and mismanagement in government. I know there were problems before, but they were able to hide it better. WHY DON'T YOU SUPPORT A MASSIVE EFFORT TO ELIMINATE WASTE, FRAUD AND MISMANAGEMENT IN THE GOVERNMENT AND DELAY OBAMASCARE A YEAR SO IT HAS A CHANCE FOR SUCCESS? COMMON SENSE HELPS ELIMINATE NO SENSE, AND NON SENSE, SO LETS TRY TO USE SOME SENSE.

Enjoy your vacation, rest your voice and breathe some fresh air maybe that will help!

August 9, 2013

President Barack Obama

1600 Pennsylvania Avenue N.W.

Washington D.C. 20500

Dear President Obama,

The elephants are not trying to destroy Obamascare, the unions, the people, the doctors, the medical industry, the IRS and the congress don't like it. Why did you grant over 1500 waivers and allow congress to bypass Obamascare? Simple, Obamascare needs more revision before it hits the market. I AGREE EVERYONE SHOULD HAVE HEALTH INSURANCE, BUT IT IS NT A GOVERNMENT PROBLEM. If you want it to be successful, delay it and fix it, I would be glad to help. Do it right or don't do it at all.

The student loan bill is a joke. Hooking interest rates to the GRANDEST CASINO IN THE WORLD is not my idea of helping the student loan program. It should be 1% interest plus honest administration costs. The future of our country doesn't need to carry a debt load on their back. It will force them to cheat and become connivers like the federal government.

Would a woman who supports abortion please tell me, with the preventative drugs and the morning after drugs, it is necessary to have abortions. I understand rape and incest, but irresponsibility by men and women, especially men, is not a good excuse to eliminate life. Maybe men should have to take a pill also.

Governor Walker fired Steven Krieser because he compared immigrants to Satan, idiot. Why does holder still have a job when he lied to congress and called Americans cowards?

You want to move the economy along, have the banks give faster decisions on foreclosures and short sales. It should not take six months for them to make up their mind. Kick them in the butt and let's get the housing market in second gear, enough is enough.

NSA surveillance and transparency do not go together. Good judgment and common sense do. The checks and balance should come from the justice department, Lord help us.

I hope you and your family enjoy your vacation, but the letters will keep coming. You can catch up on your mail when you get back.

August 10, 2013

President Barack Obama

1600 Pennsylvania Avenue N.W.

Washington D.C. 20500

Dear President Obama,

Just some notes while you are away on vacation. You promise speedy service for injured vets, so why are they looking into my approved claim instead of working on the backlog? Just a coincidence, I'm sure.

The Mexican cartels are growing marijuana on federal land in America and polluting the soil with heavy toxins and you attach legislation to the immigration bill to stop this? The bill should stand alone and not be hidden in other legislation. I don't hear anything from the environmentalist about this. They should walk the forest where the cartels have armed guards protecting their crops in national forest.

The heavy crude from Canada is being shipped by rail. How many more accidents and dead people will there have to be before you approve the pipeline. Innocent people are dying waiting on your decision. Make the decision so alternative measures can be provided to protect the people and towns from further accidents.

Senator McCaskill is a big Hillary supporter now, how convenient. I wonder what end of the jackass she talking from. There has to be another woman out there that is a better candidate than Hillary. Enough with the Clinton's, Bush's and the Palin's. Support a strong female CEO that has a proven track record. I'll vote for her.

SNAP is on the rise and so is the abuse in the program. Maybe we should remind people, it is not a way of life but a supplement to help them through tough times. Do we need some oversight here, I think so?

The Benghazi investigation is sealed, but CNN knows what is in the indictments and has interviewed the leader of the assault. That's what I call transparency, or maybe good investigative reporting. The law protects the criminals and buries the victims, good job.

August 11, 2013

President Barack Obama

1600 Pennsylvania Avenue N.W.

Washington D.C. 20500

Dear President Obama,

Holder's plan to cut federal time served and release drug offenders because the civil rights groups claim too many low income individuals are incarcerated is a slap in the face to every law abiding citizen. What about the crime and the murders their activities caused because they deal or use drugs? What about their innocent victims? If the civil rights groups want to help these people then why don't they make sure they get the proper education that will help make them successful? Why do we let young people QUIT SCHOOL? Where do you think they are going to find work without an education? Drug users are just as responsible as drug dealers. Holder's plan sucks!

What a waste of money sending letters to small businesses about cash accounting. Maybe if the government didn't waste so much money, people wouldn't keep trying to figure a way to cheat the government. Government's poor management has to be fixed and tax reform must be done. The cheater looking for other cheaters, good business.

REDUCE GOVERNMENT TO ONE SENATOR AND THREE REPRESENTATIVES FROM EVERY STATE, YOU WILL SAVE WASTED MONEY, HAVE BETTER LEGISLATION AND COOPERATIONS AMONG THE PARTIES. Fewer legislators, good legislation and private enterprise built this country, not massive, mismanaged government.

The dream nine did more to set back immigration reform than any conservative group could possibility do. They spit in the face of all Americans trying to help them, stupid.

The fraction among the elephants is saving grace for you. Can you imagine if they were all on the same page, compromise and cooperation and chicanery would disappear?

Biden over Hillary, never going to happen. Biden over anyone, never going to happen. The man does not have the silver tongue. Hillary better hope her brother's and McAuliffe's investigation goes away and Bill doesn't get in anymore trouble. She might have a chance.

Enjoy your vacation, family time is good time. Mr. President, how come I never see your golf score on the sports page?

August 12, 2013

President Barack Obama

1600 Pennsylvania Avenue N.W.

Washington D.C. 20500

Dear President Obama,

The clown in the bull ring at the Missouri State Fair should have been horned where the sun don't shine. There isn't any medication that will help stupidity and ignorance.

Judge Schiusdlin's ruling on stop and frisk is a setback for all American, especially for Americans living in poor neighborhoods. Police stop and frisk for a reason and the crime rate reduction has proven this. People that are stopped should take a moment to think that it may be their life that is saved some day by due diligence. People that have such a problem with it should never fly or enter a major sporting event. Get over IT. VICTIMS HAVE RIGHTS TO.

So you're taking a bus tour when you return from vacation. More talk, is this the best use of your time when you have fiscal legislation coming up in October. I think your staff needs more direction or we will end up with another bill like Obamascare. Stop campaigning for the donkeys and start doing your job.

The economy is doing better and the budget deficit is shrinking. Create more jobs not speeches, this will help the economy. Work on the disaster relief plan I suggested, that will create more jobs and have the insurance companies help fund it.

Obamascare must be delayed entirely. You are delaying the deductibles and copay sections of the program and have no legitimate way to verify incomes, what does that tell you. This is going to hurt the economy and the country will slide backwards again. Stop play politics with people's health. Get it right.

The states are responsible for voting rights not the federal government. The states should extend voting to two days if everyone can't get to vote in one day. Absentee ballots should be for the military, people overseas on business and the physically disabled. Photo ID should be a requirement with proof of residency. The government needs to stop diluting the responsibility of the people's right to vote. Men and women have died preserving that right. Their sacrifice shouldn't be mired by the government's inability to have HONEST elections.

Congratulations to Lieutenant General Michelle Johnson, the first woman to take charge of the Air Force Academy, be fair, firm and consistent and you will do a great job.

August 13, 2013

President Barack Obama

1600 Pennsylvania Avenue N.W.

Washington D.C. 20500

Dear President Obama,

"EDUCATION IS THE MOST POWERFUL WEAPON YOU CAN USE TO CHANGE THE WORLD" NELSON MANDELA.

It is time for people to stop looking backward and start looking forward. It is time for people to stop making excuses for why they can't do something and look for solutions to achieve their goals. The voting rights law suits are a waste of time and money. The failed education system and the entitlement programs has built the poor and low income class in this country. Congressman John Lewis's achievements are distinguishable but he lives more in the past then the future. An educated person has the ability to do what is necessary to vote in their state, they don't need special laws and excuses to drive them to the voter registration board and show the necessary documents. They do it for a drivers license, maybe voting isn't as important to them as driving.

The only cowards I see are you and Holder, who won't step up to the plate and speak the truth and do something about it. You are allowing this nation to follow their excuses and never teaching them solutions. This is a trait in all politicians. One day the blacks and Hispanics are going to figure out what you are doing to them.

Stop delaying the Fed decision hoping it won't change the election results. More excuses for not doing your job. It can't be what is right for America, it has to be what is right for democrats.

Hillary, the decision for Obamascare was alright for you but not the decision for the voting rights act, what a hypocrite. I hope another dark horse candidate comes along and takes you out of the race for president. I would have voted for you over Obama, but you and Sarah caved on the front lines.

IT IS TIME FOR THIS NATION TO STOP LOOKING BACKWARDS, MAKING EXCUSES WHY WE CAN'T DO THINGS, STOP DEPENDING ON THE GOVERNMENT, AND CREATE SOLUTIONS FOR PROSPERITY FOR ALL AMERICANS.

August 14, 2013

President Barack Obama

1600 Pennsylvania Avenue N.W.

Washington D.C. 20500

Dear President Obama,

I know you are on vacation so I will help keep you abreast of what is going on. Newt was out telling the elephants to stop picking on you and do what is necessary to help America, I agree. It is my job as an American to tell you what I think. The elephants haven't figured out chasing you is only making them look dumber than they are.

Amnesty for the immigrants, let's get it done. The people that complain the most are the people that hire them for their low wages. They are here because they wanted a better life and most of them are hard workers. Shut the borders and shut the opposition's mouth and move on with an amnesty program and a path to citizenship. THE JOBS THEY TAKE ARE JOBS THE COMPLAINERS DON'T WANT. The opponents should be more worried about the high tech visas that are issued, they are taking the jobs that should employ Americans.

Instruct the NAACP to worry more about education opportunities for their people than some clown in Missouri.

Obamascare is causing concerns with school budgets around the country. This piece of legislation is a waste of time and money as written. Delay the damn thing and fix the problems. If you need help to straighten it out I will come to Washington and do it for you. It is an insurance problem and not a government problem. Wake up, you will get the credit in the end. Delaying it would be a win, win situation for you.

Nurse practitioners should be state and federally certified and should have the same rights in every state to practice. They will be a savior for Obamascare when you fix the problems.

The inter government agreement with the Cayman Islands and the FATCA program is a good law. People that enjoy the prosperity from America should leave their money here, not overseas. However, people are tired of government waste, fraud and mismanagement so they cheat and are deceitful like the government. You are going to sneak in a tax on cell phones when Wheeler is in charge of the FCC, a perfect example.

Lois Lerner is on a path to destruction and she is going to have an impact on you sooner than you think. She didn't read the manual on how to cover her tracks and you're not too good in that department either.

August 15, 2013

President Barack Obama

1600 Pennsylvania Avenue N.W.

Washington D.C. 20500

Dear President Obama,

   Our troops are requesting items that will help save lives and maintain their health. Hagel blames it on logistic and suppliers. If we can't supply the troops, BRING THEM HOME. We are involved in a war that has been going on for thousands of years. It is better to know who your enemies are than to wonder who they are. Countries have to solve their own problems and we shouldn't be telling them what to do when we can't solve our own problems.

   The fiscal problems ahead have a simple solution, delay Obamascare, bring the troops home, leave the cuts in place, delay the debt limit legislation on a month by month basis, and do something about the waste and fraud in the government. Government and congress need to learn how to manage their money.

   HHS released 67 million for navigators, 150 million for grants to make people aware of Obamascare and took another 13 million from the disease prevention program. All this money spent on something we have been talking about for 5 years. What a waste.

   The School Standard Common Core program is a step in the right direction. It points out why we are 26th in the world in education. Standard testing proved 67% of the students couldn't pass the test. Do not adjust the standards to the weakness but bring up the performance of the teachers and the students. Stop the unions from making excuses and start finding solutions. This is a good thing you have supported, don't cave.

   Cities have to borrow money in order to open school sessions, this is another example of poor fiscal management by local, state and federal government. Let's dump some more money advertising Obamascare rather than children's education.

   The elephants should stop worrying about Hillary's movies and start worrying about their fractured party. They are getting like you when you blamed everything on Bush. I give you a better leadership grade than I give them, but neither one is that good. Start putting the needs of America first.

August 16, 2013

President Barack Obama

1600 Pennsylvania Avenue N.W.

Washington D.C. 20500

Dear President Obama,

You are going to make sure that Obamascare works and see it through to the end, and it will be the end of you and all your good intentions. The young people you conned, that helped reelect you don't want your insurance. DELAY IT AND FIX IT, then proceed with implementation. Get over this obsession.

The government is seeking a reversal on the decision for Bernanke to testify in the AIG lawsuit, and the reason it gives is it will take too much of his time, well la de da, the man will have plenty of time after he leaves office. What a lame excuse for a so called transparent administration.

HHS is giving Planned Parenthood more money after they pleaded quality and are paying a 4.3 million dollar settlement for overbilling Medicaid for women services. Hello, is anybody home at HHS. PP has cheated the federal government and the taxpayers, so let's give them a reward. Remember WASTE, FRAUD, AND MISMANAGEMENT? Now you have a company that cheated the government, promoting your key piece of legislation.

Congress wants strict oversight of the NSA, they can't manage themselves and refuse to weed out their own criminal offenders and their going to watch the NSA a spy agency, well hello, would someone wake up congress and tell them they are a spy agency and they probably have read the manual from the IRS on how to cover your tracks. Maybe they missed a chapter here and there. The blind leading the blind.

Mc Cain and Graham made some real progress on their visit to Egypt, now they want you to stop aid to Egypt after they killed over 600 people with the weapons we supplied. Is that Nobel Peace Prize medal getting a little heavy to carry? Did Susan Rice get the wrong talking points to pass on to them before their trip?

Car 54 where are you, oh, in area 51, the CIA finally found you. The world is laughing at this revelation, we found area 51, what a spy agency, and it's in our country. So, who stroked up these talking points?

The two key points to getting into the country, you ask for asylum and you're staying at the Holiday Inn, and you wonder why people are angry about illegal immigrants!

August 17, 2013

President Barack Obama

1600 Pennsylvania Avenue N.W.

Washington D.C. 20500

Dear President Obama,

The tax code needs to be reformed when it is a major cause of middle income people renouncing their citizenship. The code should have been reformed long ago and is the driver that forces people and businesses to cheat on their taxes. Of course, you can't reform this code unless you reform the governments waste, fraud and mismanagement.

I wonder why congress has let the executive branch take so much power away from it. The executive branch has over reached its power through executive orders and spends money without congressional approval. The president is a border line dictator and he acts like one. The state governments should recall their senators and representatives and stop paying taxes to the federal government until the decision is made, do we support the constitution and the bill of rights or not. Federal government is out of control, it is time to stop them.

The jackasses are outraged over NSA security leaks, this is a joke. Where is their outrage over fast and furious, Benghazi, the IRS scandal and the 400 surface to air missiles that are missing? Very soon they will be complaining about no toilet paper in the bathrooms. Oh well, WHAT DOES IT MATTER.

Larry Summers was voted out as the President of Harvard by his peers because he made disparaging remarks about women and minorities intelligence, so why the hell is Obama considering this man for the Federal Reserve job? The stock market reacts to what the leader of the Fed does and this man is a loose cannon and a Wall Street manipulator. He was part of the 2008 collapse and ran off to Harvard and they kicked him out, so back to Wall Street.

Mr. President, overall if you used more common sense than democratic sense, you would probably go down as being one of the greatest Presidents, however that is not the case. You sold your soul to the jackass and that is the correlative value of your administration. IT IS NOT TOO LATE TO PUT AMERICA FIRST, IT JUST TAKES GUTS.

August 18, 2013

President Barack Obama

1600 Pennsylvania Avenue N.W.

Washington D.C. 20500

Dear President Obama,

I suggested long ago for you to put together a national response team that could put out forest fires and respond to other national disasters, this idea has fallen on deaf ears. Barbara Boxer is complaining about global warming as if we will be able to change any damage that has been done, but she fails to solve the problems. Putting out the fire is the important problem, not worrying about global warming. The last time I checked it took a match or lighting to start a fire. You will never be able to control the carelessness of people, but you will be able to stop a fire if you dedicate enough equipment and men when it starts. The insurance companies will financially support such a program. It is cheaper to stop a fire than payout claims. Wake up in Washington. A national program will ensure that all fire fighters families have the same benefits.

You can tell Elliot Pulham to stop being a girly man about NASA missing a meeting because of a budget cut to travel. Maybe he should think of the twenty million people without a job. Has he ever heard of teleconference or he too far in space. Get over it.

Meeting with the finance regulators is a joke. Three years later and they only have completed 39% of the required work. Government at work. Are they on the bonus list?

You have a major drought problem in the west. What is being done about that? Maybe we should wait till Lake Mead dries up and we can use it for a land fill. It is a problem that you need to have some input and not blame it on global warming. Maybe the USA can't support any more population out west? I know the states have been arguing about it but nothing is getting done.

Supplying weapons to the Middle East has done nothing but kill their people, kill American military, replace any kind of law with disorder, and become a major financial drain. Approve the pipeline so we do not have to depend on any oil from the Middle East and let them solve their own problems for now. Give them a chance to do something on their own without our interference. Other than our money, I can't see why anyone would solicit our advice when we have so many problems at home. Minding our own business could be a good thing.

Welcome back from vacation and stop blaming the republicans for your problems. They can't help themselves and you piling it on won't help, the same goes for the democrats. ARE THERE ANY AMERICANS LEFT IN WASHINGTON?

August 19, 2013

President Barack Obama

1600 Pennsylvania Avenue N.W.

Washington D.C. 20500

Dear President Obama,

You meant with the financial regulators and express your sense of urgency regarding the slow progress they are making. It has been three years since the Dodd Frank law was passed and they have only completed 40% of the work. The original bill was 835 pages and they have added over 13,000 pages of regulations. The sense of urgency you should exercise is to fire these regulators for lack of performance. With their lack of performance, can you really trust what they have put in those 13,000 pages of regulations? This will not get you the Nobel Prize in economics.

There are 106,000 people in New Jersey that are covered with a basic and essential health care policy. They will lose this coverage because the policy does not meet the minimum standards set in Obamascare. You stated, "People can keep their current policies," the law you signed states they cannot keep their policy. You did not read the 2700 page law you signed and your staff gave you the wrong talking points. The truth of the matter is you are using Obamascare to help produce a single payer system that you wanted from the start. This is going to cost you dearly and you will ruin your democratic party. Maybe they will even vote you out like they did to Larry Summers, who lost his job as President of Harvard.

The Head Start Program for children is suffering financial cut because of the sequester you used as a bargaining chip that backfired. Stop the free cell phone program that you and the previous president have started and use the 2.1 billion dollars you wasted on that program. Simple, stop that program and redistribute the money where it will do some good. Why did Carlos Slim, from Mexico, receive over 500 million in profit from that program? I guess there wasn't an American company that could have profited from the program. It could have been run better and not cost as much, more waste and the money went to a billionaire.

Representatives Barcus and Camp are working on a tax reform bill that could eliminate the tax break for municipal and state bonds. Barcus wrote a majority of Obamascare and declared it was going to be a train wreck if it isn't fixed and now he is working on tax reform. What is wrong with this picture? I'll help, this is a potential fiscal bombshell to the bond market and the local governments that depend on bonds for educational improvements. Welcome home!

August 20, 2013

President Barack Obama

1600 Pennsylvania Avenue N.W.

Washington D.C. 20500

Dear President Obama,

So Ace, you finally found a Miami Dolphin. It only took you forty years, this obviously is a great use of your time when there are so many other important issues to worry about. Besides, I doubt if they played football just so they could come to the Whitehouse, there must have been greater rewards.

Why are people so shocked that the NSA is spying on people, which is their job? Do people think the enemy is going to huddle in one spot and wave a flag, here we are. Kids and adults are sitting in a park sucking on marijuana, do you think they might be a security risk?

Benghazi, all the suspended people were reinstated in other jobs, what does it matter. The only thing phony about this scandal is the way your administration is handling it. CNN and the Wall Street Journal have interviewed the mastermind and what has your administration done, changed names to protect the GUILTY. Could you be guilty of a cover up? SHAMEFUL!

You, Mc Cain and Graham deserve each other, you can't figure out who is on first base in Egypt. Give them aid, no don't give them aid, no just give them bullets, no give them money to buy Russian bullets, no they are American weapons so they need our bullets, give them the bullets the social security fund purchased, no lets stand on the fence a little longer. Get off the fence, you know you will be happy if they disband the Muslin Brotherhood, maybe not you Mr. President, but it would be a good thing if you finally know who your friend is over there.

Major fires in the west, a water shortage problem in the west, marijuana being grown in the national forest, second hand smoke from the Seattle Park polluting the air, Barbara Boxer worried about global warming when this has been the coolest August in California, the Fed ready to pull back on bond purchases, health insurance increased by 4%, Ted Cruz worried about Obamascare and his Canadian citizenship, AND YOUR GOING ON A BUS TOUR! The Oval Office is not there for picture opportunities, it is your work place or cubicle. Report to work.

Be sure to tell the students, as the economy gets better, your interest rates will go up on your school loans. What a genius move that is!

August 21, 2013

President Barack Obama

1600 Pennsylvania Avenue N.W.

Washington D.C. 20500

Dear President Obama,

The fires out west are out of control and out of money to pay the firefighters. The National Forestry Agency is transferring funds from other budgets to pay for these efforts. The problem gets worse every year and to date 697 million dollars have been spent trying to put these fires out. These fires need to be put out at inception not weeks later or waiting for the winds to change or rain. I suggested many times that a National Disaster Team, with the right equipment should be established to help local officials put these fires out in their early stage. We have enough equipment in mothballs that can be regenerated, to give the fire fighters a greater edge. This would be money well spent and the insurance companies can contribute.

Marijuana, if you don't stop demand at the street level, you will never solve the problem. Jailing pushers and traffickers is a temporary measure because there is always someone ready to take their place. Put a high mandatory fine and immediate time in jail on users to stem the tide. Not enforcing the law is giving the dealers a license to operate and kill thousands of people along the way. Everyone who smokes or does drugs should wonder who they killed that day so they could suck on a joy stick. If we are a society of laws, then they should be enforced.

Josh Earnest needs a reality check. Three out of every four jobs are part time. Young adults are working to pay their bills, the high cost of food and gas and use their discretionary money for entertainment, not health insurance. It seems that fun and good times take president over Obamascare. Many of them use their money for fitness centers and the social network that offers. Obamascare is evaporated money like car insurance, you only really want it when you need it. So Josh, hit yourself in the head with a pillow and wake up.

Mr. President, do yourself a favor and skip the speech at the Lincoln Memorial. Are people of color better off today than they were 50 years ago, they don't think so. They think you can legislate them to success, but that will never be the solution. Education and moral values is the path to success, not legislation and entitlements. That will always be a problem for them as long as we remain 26th in the world in education. I never hear anyone refer to you as the Black Mr. President, but I always hear people refer to themselves as black, Hispanic, Italian, Asian and many other prefixes, but not, I AM AN AMERICAN. Ronald Reagan knew that was the thread sewed our great country together. You and the political parties have shredded that legacy.

August 22, 2013

President Barack Obama

1600 Pennsylvania Avenue N.W.

Washington D.C. 20500

Dear President Obama,

The last meeting, with your administration, regarding the fiscal crisis was August 1st. Did everyone go one vacation and the bus ride with you? So now what do the American people get, another rush job like Obamascare was. Talk is really cheap in Washington, all of you should be ashamed of yourselves.

Before you ride around the country pushing a value rating for colleges, why don't you evaluate congress, the senate and your administration? Let me do it for you, a lazy, dismal bunch of egotistical jackasses and elephants that produce legislation that resembles DUNG. You have a nerve even thinking about evaluating a politicalized education system. You measure their value by how many of their challenged students graduate and what level of success they have in the work place. The system Arne Duncan proposes will lend itself to creative mathematical results. The biggest joke is he will seek input from congress.

Syria has used chemical weapons, probably from Iraq, since they crossed the red line, what are you going to do? Let me suggest that you call the generals in Egypt from the bus and tell them to organize an air strike. You might also call Saudi officials, after all they could be Syria's next targets. Let that region solve its own problems.

Holder's attack on states voting right because he didn't like the Supreme Court's decision is wrong and a waste of money. How is this discrimination when half the country doesn't get off their butts to vote? If everyone voted, you wouldn't be President. Look at the math, 15% Hispanic, mostly undocumented, about 15% black, the rest white and other and an unknown number of declared Americans like me, you lose. If you can't get off your butt to get an ID and go vote then we deserve the government we have. I am more worried about the intelligence of the voter and if they are being held hostage by entitlements, aren't you? I don't think so!

If you are really worried about education, you need to start from the bottom up. The poor in this country are getting the short end of the stick. You keep pumping money into a poor education system. The system needs to be fixed and the money needs to be spent the right way. When you and Holder are ready to talk race relations seriously, I will be happy to help you with this problem. I say again, "Education is the most powerful weapon we can use to change the world," NELSON MANDELLA. Look in the mirror and maybe you can see what it did for you.

August 23, 2013

President Barack Obama

1600 Pennsylvania Avenue N.W.

Washington D.C. 20500

Dear President Obama,

Your statement, "economic troubles have cause racial and class divisions," is partially correct, so what are you doing on a bus tour hyping Biden for President. What is the point of going to college if you can't find a job when you graduate? The economy should be your number one priority and the coming fiscal legislation that your administration hasn't had a meeting about since August 1st. Get your priorities in order.

The elephants are worried about backlash from the fiscal talks and the jackasses are worried about your legacy, so who is worried about America. The elephant creed, cut spending, no cut waste, fraud, and poor management is a better approach. The jackasses are worried if they manage entitlements better they will lose votes. I never hear the words efficiency and fiscal responsibility used in Washington in the same sentence. It is all about getting reelected. Dah, that's not why you're there.

You cannot legislate racial equality. Only education and success will do that. This DHS employee that set up the racial website calling for blacks to kill white people is on paid leave. This is a slap in the face to all Americans. Just so this jerk knows, bad people come in all colors, class, and ethnicities and the same goes for all good people. The business world wants the best person for the jobs they have, the government wants fills their jobs based on percentages and not qualifications. Their efforts to help the poor class is a dismal failure fueled by the poor education system. Government measures their success by votes, not results.

You can keep your doctor and your medical plan, but I forgot to tell you, because of the regulation we put on businesses they might drop you from your insurance plan. Well, Mr. President, which is exactly what is happening. Over 500 groups, businesses, and lobby organizations are asking you to change things. Your legacy is more important than doing what is right for America. Man up, delay the plan, fix it or set the standards and have the insurance industry provide the solution. It is really their problem, not a government problem.

You put yourself in a box with Syria, why don't you have are so called friends in the Middle East solve the problem for you? Why do we have to be the good guy all the time? Syria is more of a threat to Europe and the Middle East than it is to America, but I know it's about oil and the Suez Canal. Sign the pipeline bill and get oil independence. Simple solution.

August 24, 2013

President Barack Obama

1600 Pennsylvania Avenue N.W.

Washington D.C. 20500

Dear President Obama,

You need to ask Eric Holder for his resignation. "I wouldn't be AG without '63 March." The legislation for the Civil Rights Bill was already being debated in the Congress and the Senate before the march took place. These facts might refresh his and your memory. It is right to honor Martin Luther King, but you have to get the facts right and give credit to the proper people.

April 3, 1963 Fred Sutterlesworth organizes the Birmingham Campaign with lunch counter sit-ins, mass meetings, direct actions, March on City Hall, and a boycott of the white merchants. King also participated and preached nonviolence, but Fred Sutterlesworth was the driving force. Sutterlesworth's home was bombed that night.

April 10, 1963 the city government obtained a court injunction to stop the demonstrations but King and the other leaders decided to be arrested and continue with the demonstrations.

April 11, 1963 King and Ralph Abernathy were arrested, but there was no bail money available to release them. King was not allowed to call his wife in Atlanta so she contacted the Kennedy Administration and King was allowed to call home and money was made available for his release on April 20, 1963.

May 2, 1963, James Bevel organized the Children's Crusade and over 1,000 students participated on a daily basis. Hundreds were arrested and Commissioner Conner ordered the police and fire department to use force. National TV coverage showed the children being abused and on one march Sutterlesworth was injured and hospitalized.

May 6, 1963 King assured the parents the children would be alright and the demonstrations continued.

There was pressure from the white owned businesses and pressure on the Whitehouse. Robert Kennedy sent Burke Marshall to negotiate with the civil rights leaders and the city government. Marshall convinced King to halt the demonstrations and he agreed without consulting Sutterlesworth who was still in the hospital.

May 8, 1963 King called off the demonstration and Sutterlesworth was furious with him. He also warned if negotiations did not produce results that the demonstrations would start again.

May 10, 1963 the Birmingham Truce Agreement was endorsed and King, Abernathy, and Sutterlesworth made the announcement. That same night a bomb went off near the motel where King and other leaders had their meetings. The next day King's brother's home was bombed. This prompted President Kennedy to move 3,000 troops just outside Birmingham.

Kennedy knew he would need republican support so on June 11, 1963 President Kennedy met with the republican leaders to discuss the bill before he announced his Civil Rights legislation on a televised speech to the nation. Two days later Majority Leader Senator Mike Mansfield and Minority Leader Senator Everett Dirksen announced their support of the bill. This was over two months before the March on Washington took place.

June 19, 1963 the President sent his bill to the House and on to the Judiciary Committee where they added stronger language and amendments. Kennedy called the house leaders in October to move the bill along and in November it moved to the rules committee despite opposition from the democrats. Kennedy was assassinated later that month but Johnson wanted the bill passed to honor Kennedy and bullied the Congress and Senate to get the job done. Howard W. Smith, a democrat from Virginia vowed to keep the bill in the Rules Committee and it remained there until after winter recess. Pressure from public opinion in the North caused Smith to relent and it moved to the Senate floor. Mansfield and Dirksen maneuvered the bill past Senator Eastland and the Judiciary Committee, a staunch opponent of the bill. The southern DEMOCRATS did their best to stop the bill with a 57 day filibuster when Senators Humphrey, Kuchel, Dirksen, and Mansfield introduced a substitute bill that stopped the filibuster and the bill passed the Senate on June 19, 1964. This was the first successful cloture vote in 37 years.

August 28, 1963 was the March on Washington. That did not stop the filibuster or the Southern Democrats from trying to stop the bill. It was a good compromise between Mansfield and Dirksen that moved the bill to President Johnson signing it on July 2, 1964. During this process there were other incidents in the south that moved public opinion.

September 15, 1963 the KKK bombed the Sixteenth Street Baptist Church and killed four young girls.

September 18, 1963 King delivered the eulogy honoring the girls as heroines of a holy crusade for freedom and human dignity.

People like Fred Sutterlesworth, Rosa Parks, and many other brave Americans brought about the Civil Rights Bill. Too many paid with their life in a Christian nation. Mr. President and Eric Holder are the recipients of the courage of many dedicated people long before the March on Washington. They received a good education that many other poor people don't have and they made it work for them. They are not making it work for other poor Americans, but they are trying to legislate their dependency on the government. You have to wonder how a Christian and civilized nation took almost 200 years to understand the words in the Declaration of Independence that all men are created equal, meaning equality for every human being?

August 25, 2013

President Barack Obama

1600 Pennsylvania Avenue N.W.

Washington D.C. 20500

Dear President Obama,

The voting rights lawsuits that Holder is filing are smoke and mirrors and just a way to antagonize the states and get the minority voters upset. If you and Holder were really worried about the right to vote, you would pass a law that the states would have in person voting at least 3 day a week, one day being a Saturday or Sunday. They should be required to have photo ID and proof of citizenship. Prisoners and convicted felons should lose their right to vote since they proved they have flawed judgment, white collar or blue collar. This is a brazen approach to voting for federal elections, but one day to vote is too short and Absentee ballots should only be for the military. If a person is going to be out of the state of residence then they should go to the voting regulators in person with plans of their trip to receive a onetime absentee ballot. Disabled people should supply proof of medical disability with their application for an absentee ballot.

This approach is restricting but it is nothing compared to the men and women that gave their lives so American citizens could have the right to vote. The excuse that you don't like either candidate can be resolved by writing in yourself or your choice. Maybe more people would vote if they had more time to do it, but that is not your goal. I believe you would rather build phantom voters to suit your needs and every state has them. The proof is evident by all the dead people that receive entitlements in the millions of dollars.

Obamascare is layered with costs before the patient gets the appropriate medical care. The IRS is involved, Navigators are involved, organizations like Plan Parenthood are involved, the IRS has hired E Health INC to qualify people for tax subsidies, the insurance companies will have to enroll these people, claims will have to be approved before treatment and the doctors and medical groups will have to hire professionals to collect their money. All of these layers are costly and the patient hasn't even seen the doctor yet. What is left for the medical professionals? TOO MUCH PAPER PROFIT AND NOT ENOUGH PROFIT FOR THE MEDICAL TREATMENT.

Delay the program, eliminate the paper profit as much as possible. I have stated it before that the government should set standards and leave it to the insurance companies to cover people on a national level, not regional. Your track record of blaming others isn't going to work here as you have been warned by the unions, businesses, politicians, the medical industry and the people.

August 26, 2013

President Barack Obama

1600 Pennsylvania Avenue N.W.

Washington D.C. 20500

Dear President Obama,

Take your time regarding the situation in Syria. We are not the world's policemen. The leaders in that region must step up to the plate. What is more important is that we support the right rebel group that will coincide with our views. The attack is over and nothing can be done to change that, but the future of the country is more important. We don't need another Egypt.

Congratulations to Ty Carter, the Medal of Honor recipient. He is the measure of the type of people you need in your administration. I know you are getting the heat for not having enough women in high level positions and frankly I would rather work with women, but you hire who you want because it's your butt on the line.

Online filing for benefits is unacceptable. Person to person, with proper documentation, is the only procedure to follow for all distribution of benefits and entitlements. People that are physically disabled should have home visits. The country is paying too many dead and imprisoned people benefits in the millions of dollars. Small inroads into waste and fraud are not acceptable.

You and every legitimate leader in the Civil Rights movement should be embarrassed to stand up before thousands of people and tell them to keep dreaming. Their government is 16 trillion dollars in debt and not much of it was spent on them to improve their lot in life. The government has failed miserably to educate and protect the children in Martin Luther King's Dream. The government has tried to legislate their success leaving out hard work and the can do attitude in the formula.

Make it against the law for gangs and clubs whose intent is criminal to exist. If expression is part of the First Amendment so should intent be a part of the First Amendment. It is a shame that our children need safe passage routes and armed guards as part of their education. I can't remember a President that has met this challenge successfully.

The Treasury Department will hit the debt limit by mid-October. Maybe you should call congress back early and solve this problem. The speeches you give at the march will not make any difference until you get everyone on board to solve that problem. It should be an integral part of the upcoming fiscal negotiations. Find the leaders in the house and senate and make it happen, the rest of the sheep will follow. Stop the feel good moments and start the real good moments.

August 27, 2013

President Barack Obama

1600 Pennsylvania Avenue N.W.

Washington D.C. 20500

Dear President Obama,

Obamascare is not a civil right as you claim. Driving is not a civil right. Gangs and clubs whose intent is criminal activity is not a civil right. Smoking marijuana is not a civil right, but this feckless government allows it to happen. Civil rights were guaranteed to the children and citizens of Newtown, Colorado, Fort Hood, Benghazi, Chicago, Detroit, and the entire nation. The laws are protecting the criminals and burying the victims.

How can you stand where King stood when you stated that race does matter, class does matter, rich versus poor does matter, and that what you want matters most. Blacks and Latinos made their greatest strides during the Reagan and Clinton years and are continuing on that path. The problem is the poor, no matter what color they are, are still left behind. You and every politician use these people and make false promises of better life to come. The political ads in this country are fracturing this country. You will talk about civil rights, but you forget one thing, you can't legislate people's success. King believed in America, but forgot to tell the people that it's elections that matter, not Americans.

Your meeting with the black faith leaders, and Holder and Jarrett is a sham. If Obamascare was such a great piece of legislation, why are you begging for help from the people to implement it? It doesn't come close to Social Security and Medicare, which congress has on track for destruction. I hope Obamascare is a resounding success, but you need to delay and fix it or it will be the cross you bear for the rest of your life.

Larry Summers is not the right man for the job. Your own party is telling you that, but you are stuck in a rut. He brings nothing to the table but criticism and bad advice. He was a part of the 2008 financial collapse and is not known for his diplomacy. You have enough bad advice already, you don't need more.

Syria is a Middle East problem. Where are the war ships and ground support from the bordering nations? What happened there is a travesty, but who helped them with the technology and weapons? Why isn't Russia sending help? Aren't you and Putin Buddies? Sometimes we say things with good intentions and they backfire. I don't know if blowing up the country and leaving is the best path to a solution. Think before you act.

August 28, 2013

President Barack Obama

1600 Pennsylvania Avenue N.W.

Washington D.C. 20500

Dear President Obama,

The food stamp program hasn't taught the government a lesson regarding fraud and mismanagement of the debit cards they use, now you are going to give these cards to people so they can pay for health benefits and services. Convenience is not always the best thing, sometimes we have to keep constraints on people's behavior. Doing this is only going to ruin Obamascare faster than you are doing it now.

You drew a line in the sand and Syria crossed it. The ramifications of your comment, no matter how noble, will cause economic hardships on America, especially the poor and middle class, will cause Israel to suffer at the hands of this mad man, will destroy a nation sending the refugees to other nations, and will cause other retaliatory strikes. It will not end with one enemy action. Assad is the problem, he must go, not innocent people. After the strike he will still be there, so what is the point of all this if the problem is never rectified. If you don't want to kill him, snatch him and lock him up.

You made some very good points at the march. You will never achieve economic equality thru legislation and you fail to change the education system of the poor and low income class. Look what your education has done for you, however you need to focus it in the right direction. CHILDREN CAN NOT LEARN IN A THREATENED AND DISRUPTIVE ENVIRONMENT. The bad and I can't do attitudes need to be separated from normal school operations. Teachers are not babysitters and referees. The environment children go home to needs to be changed. Safe passage routes are not the answer, safe environments is the answer. The laws keep protecting the criminals and burying our children physically and economically.

Stop the lawsuits and blaming the states voting laws claiming civil rights violations. Any person no matter what color they are will have to go through the same process and have the proper identification to vote. They do it to get a driver's license, so what the hell is the problem.

You will never fix America's problems until you fix the problems in Washington. There are 535 legislators, 9 judges, a president and his staff and a warped judicial system down line. Who is in charge of this circus, all I ever hear or read is you can't do this, you have to talk to me

first, I'll shut down the government if you don't compromise, this is a violation of the Constitution, and who cares the Constitution is out dated. Well I care and so should you.

August 29, 2013

President Barack Obama

1600 Pennsylvania Avenue N.W.

Washington D.C. 20500

Dear President Obama,

Where exactly does it state in the Constitution which laws can be enforced and which laws cannot be enforced. The baby that was left in a hot car, in Arizona, and died because the father was high on marijuana is one of many victims that will suffer from the government's lack of action. I guess your voting legislation is more important than a child's life.

Your message on shoring up the middle class is wrong as usual. How can you have a strong economical foundation built on the poor and low income people? They must be reinforced through education and success. Foundations are built from the bottom up, not the top down. Education is the strength of a nation, not legislation.

The department of education is issuing waivers on no child left behind. This is because the states have demonstrated their ability to provide a better education for their children. The law expired and congress is working on a new law. Instead of supporting foreign student, why don't we put federal schools in states that have a high number of at risk student, bad attitude and mentally challenged students and deal with each level accordingly? These will be dormitory supported so the students don't have to go back into the same environment that is creating the problem. It is based on every child has worth and potential, they just need the right professional direction to help them. Too many teachers are babysitters and referees that needs to stop.

This is hilarious, we are suing the Swiss banks because people are hiding their money in Swiss bank accounts. This is a blatant failure of our archaic and complicated tax code. We are punishing another nation for our lack of control and organization and this magnifies the waste, fraud and mismanagement of our government. Why do you think people and companies cheat on their taxes, because they are tired of seeing the government waste it?

A meeting at the White House, with the magical eight republicans, produced no results on the fiscal negotiations. A strike on Syria will make our poor suffer the most. Think about it.

Susan Rice, who are the good guys and who are the bad guys, do we know? The President should be briefing congress and the senate, not Susan Rice. This could be another Bay of Tomkins Resolution that escalated the Vietnam War. Thousands of people are dying in the Middle East everyday, why is this incident so important? Is it ok to kill someone with a bomb, or a bullet, or a knife, dead is dead. Is how they die more important than just dying?

August 30, 2013

President Barack Obama

1600 Pennsylvania Avenue N.W.

Washington D.C. 20500

Dear President Obama,

    The magical eight republicans picked up their marbles and went home after a nonproductive meeting with your chief of staff on the budget crisis. The republicans want to restructure the federal benefits programs, reform the tax code, and cut unnecessary spending, your administration wants to raise taxes. During these discussions they should put a big sign on the wall, Detroit and San Bernardino in bankruptcy. First it will be the towns, next it will be the states and last it will be the country if we don't do something about our national debt. Raising taxes when so many people are out of work and the cost of living is going up is not the answer.

    An attack on Syria carries many risks with it. The cost of living will go up because of the oil prices, the SEA, Syrian Electronic Army which has hacked the NY Times and papers in Britain promises major interruptions against any aggressors, the neighboring allies will suffer the most if Syria decides to retaliate, and all this is supported by physical and circumstantial evidence, some of it very damning and questionable.

    There are over 100,000 dead from this civil war and many more injured, why are we acting now when if we were really concerned we should have acted in the beginning. We are over involved in the Middle East and always in a no win situation. Egypt is in chaos, Iraq is suffering civil unrest and killings, Afghanistan is no better off now than when the Russians left it, and we have never learned to manage our affairs in that region after all our involvement. We deliver weapons to that region and then we complain because they use them against each other. Every country must find its own level of stability, no matter how liberal or religiously restrictive.

    America, as great as we are, is not a shining example of democracy all the time, especially in our financial matters. We have very similar problems, but are more civil about them in most cases. Mr. President, we are who we are and you don't have to prove it to our friends or enemies. Don't be bullied into a conflict that can spin out of control and cause major repercussions for America and our allies. It is time to earn the Nobel Peace Prize you were awarded.

August 31, 2013

President Barack Obama

1600 Pennsylvania Avenue N.W.

Washington D.C. 20500

Dear President Obama,

It isn't very often I agree with you on your decisions, but you have made the right move on Syria both politically and in the best interest of our allies. No one is taking credit for the gas attacks, so most of the evidence, other than physical, is circumstantial. You don't know which of the three rebel groups fighting Assad are committed to democracy as we know it and neither does anyone else. You must reconsider leaving Assad in power. The two wars in Iraq are a perfect example of when you don't cut the head off the snake. You need more time and intellengce boots on the ground to determine what the future will be, it makes no sense to replace a snake with a snake.

Politically, the big mouths in Washington that want their say should get it and suffer the ramifications of it. You ought to give Cameron a kiss on the cheek for giving you a way out of the box you put yourself in. Your intentions, though noble, carry too many consequences for the Syrians, Americans, and all our allies. This was a profile in courage moment and you were able to get the monkey off your back at the same time. Inadvertently slick?

Obamascare, if the elephants spent as much time trying to fix the problem with Obamascare as they have trying to destroy it, maybe we would have a plan that will actually work. The jackasses are no help because they haven't come up with any solutions either. Delay the program, remove all the wavers, inform the senate, congress and all federal employees they will be a part of the program like everyone else, set minimum standards for the insurance companies and make the coverage and sales nationwide, not state to state, and let the insurance companies and the medical industry come up with the solution and congress to fix the equality issues. Everyone pays, coverage is equitable, and the government will commit to subsidies after reviewing the insurance companies plans. The second part of the equation is the people need to know that their personal responsibility in health care will impact individual premiums that they have control over, for example most cases of obesity. You made one good decision now make another.

Small notes, Iraq citizens are protesting the generous benefits and pensions that the legislators are giving themselves, why isn't that a surprise. Instruct the scientific community to come up with solutions for the radioactive water that is leaking into the ocean by Japan.

September 1, 2013

President Barack Obama

1600 Pennsylvania Avenue N.W.

Washington D.C. 20500

Dear President Obama,

   Recently, I post my letters to you on my web site and others hoping they are informative and suggestive to different ideas. I found a web site, Little Green Footballs, and posted some of my letters. I was not sure of the nature of the web site until communication started to flow. The group I communicated with were ardent, intelligent supporters of you. This was clearly not a path to follow from someone who is critical of your administration and you. The exchanges were pleasant, curt, intelligent and sometimes accusatory, normal for different points of view.

   There were exchanges indicating my dislike for you, so I need to set the record straight. I stated on more than one occasion, in different forums, you are a charismatic individual and a good family man. My critique of you is based on your performance as I see it, not your adversaries. I don't spend hours writing these letters just to bash you. I credit you with your good decisions, am puzzled by other decisions, and continue to think you put party over country. I respect you as a man and as the President, but in my exchanges with the Little Green Footballs I find it necessary to adjust my parameters on your performance.

   Intermittently, we clashed all day on information, resources, party affiliations, and viewpoints. It was a tug a war and a suggestion was made that I might want to find a friendlier web site. I realized our exchanges were not going anywhere fast toward common ground. I was dealing with several individuals without measurable results. I can imagine what you must feel like dealing with congress, the senate, and 535 opinions, all thinking they are right. I will continue to communicate with The Little Footballs and hope that we can build a level of trust that doesn't need to be supported by links and resources. I respect their opinions and feelings and hope they will reciprocate.

   The Little Footballs are right about one thing, the republicans are always using threatening legislation when positive compromise should be an option. However, the democrats continue to push for tax hikes that hurt the poor and middle class more than the rich. The rich will always be rich and the poor and middle class will always suffer from any tax increase. The cost always go downhill and very seldom are absorbed at the top. Trust, common goals and compromise are the answer and there isn't a math formula for that, only leadership.

September 2, 2013

President Barack Obama

1600 Pennsylvania Avenue N.W.

Washington D.C. 20500

Dear President Obama,

You have put yourself in the corner on this Syrian situation. I admire your courage, but this could be a political disaster for you and future legislation. Besides Obamascare, you have presented a controversy to congress that has democrats and republicans reeling against you. This could compromise your position on the budget and Obamascare issues facing congress. Unfortunately, the approval you are seeking on Syria is going to cost you measurable political capital. I hope congress has enough sense to deal with each issue on its own merits and doesn't use one to gain advantage over another as they usually do.

The Middle East has been a cross to bear for every President and even with our major involvement there, democracy is not rooting well. Religious beliefs will always deter this from happening no matter how many young people want change. We have dumped billions of dollars in that region to secure peace and it has produced nothing tangible other than Israel. You can't use them as a shining example because the rest of the Middle East hates them and us.

I don't see Russia or China offering any support. They would object to anything we do just to see us debate this issue and make fools of ourselves, and with a fractured congress this will likely be the outcome. A concession I would make is Assad has to go as part of a deal. It makes no sense to leave him in power. We have to align ourselves with the right rebel group, if there is a right rebel group, if not, this is just the humanitarian thing to do.

Israel has the most to lose in any scenario other than us doing nothing and that is a possibility. They are living under a stronger threat than Syria right now and I suppose they are accustomed to this by now, but it has to be unnerving waiting for our fractured congress to decide their fate and the people in Syria.

I am sure you have considered all these points and the problems you will have with congress. I would have supported an immediate strike rather than go through this current process. You will need a little luck and strong leadership in this endeavor.

September 3, 2013

President Barack Obama

1600 Pennsylvania Avenue N.W.

Washington D.C. 20500

Dear President Obama,

   You have scheduled meetings with China, France and other world leaders, why not Putin? Russia is supplying the weapons and has a major influence with Assad. It's not too late to have a face to face meeting with Assad and Putin and try to resolve this problem. I am sure that there have been low level meetings with Assad, but before you commit to this limited military strike, which will not be limited and it doesn't take a genius to figure that out, ask Putin to stop weapon deliveries and arrange a meeting. Self-interest groups, like the American Syrian groups and the war hawks in congress are pushing for this action. If there is any chance of a peaceful resolution, it should be explored. There is no conclusive evidence who used the gas, just that it was used.

   The senate and congress should be more concerned with our looming budget crisis and the foolish maneuvers they might try to eliminate Obamascare. Obamascare should be delayed and fixed to assure that it will be a solid functioning solution to the American people and the medical industry. Except for the fraud and waste, Medicare is Obamascare for the elderly. The idea that this should be a single payer system goes against group discounts, family coverage, and common business sense. This is and will always be an insurance industry problem. The simple fact that Medicare is contracted out to medical groups is evidence the government can't operate it efficiently. Take Obamascare out of the budget process, push for the minimum wage increase and the immigration program. Have the medical and insurance industry fix Obamascare.

   To all the people that have a problem with giving the immigrants amnesty, get over it, they are here and performing jobs that you wouldn't do or let your children do. To the immigrants, if you are here just for the dollar, go home. To the government, it is your job to sort out the good, the bad and the immigrants that want to be American and contribute to society. Ship the bad out, give work visas to the applicable and start a realistic path for citizenship for the people that want to stay. It isn't a complicated process. While you're at it, put a high tax on companies that require tech visas for foreign employees. If they want them that bad over Americans, make them pay for it.

   Mr. President, the railroad lobbyist are trying to delay the Train Safety legislation, don't let that happen. The federal laws governing marijuana should be enforced, it's not optional.

September 4, 2013

President Barack Obama

1600 Pennsylvania Avenue N.W.

Washington D.C. 20500

Dear President Obama,

The policy relaxing the immigration laws regarding American children of immigrant parents is coherent with our stand on human rights. Immigration control starts at the border. Our efforts to find and control immigrants in the country and what to do with them is lack luster and contradictory. Doing a better job of securing the border is the first step and using employee e file, done right, would be the next step. The business community could help themselves and the immigrants at the same time. Hospitals would be another point of assistance.

The budget, debt limit, immigration legislation, the appointment of the fed chairperson and the examination of the surveillance laws are all taking a back seat to the Syrian Resolution that the majority of the American people are against. More effort is being wasted on this, when Obamacare needs the attention and review as well as the other pending legislation. Congress has taken 239 days off the calendar leaving the legislative process short changed. Priorities?

What makes you and your staff think, that a leader who has killed over 100,000 of his own people, isn't going to retaliate against his neighbors and us. I agree something has to be done about Syria, but without Russia and China's support and doing a limited strike, it is like spitting into the wind. The best option would be to target him and his staff and not ruin the infrastructure that 2,000,000 refugees might return too. There is also the question of what rebel group will seize power? If we had more intelligence boots on the ground, this decision may be a better option. This strike is too risky and all a downside for America.

What is Obamacare going to do to the poor class that have no insurance and have to buy it or pay a penalty at tax time? If a poor person is accepted into Medicaid, will they still have to pay a penalty on their taxes because they do not have insurance through Obamacare? Illegal immigrants are not covered by Obamacare now and this will continue to drive up the cost. What determines if a person is eligible for Obamacare or Medicaid? Too many unanswered questions. I still support a delay until it will be implemented properly. This isn't going to happen, so Americans, get ready for a bumpy ride the President talked about. I just hope we don't hit any sinkholes.

Defense training for the Myanmar Army, a country that has done what Syria is doing and much worse, doesn't make any sense. You should rethink your position on this.

September 5, 2013

President Barack Obama

1600 Pennsylvania Avenue N.W.

Washington D.C. 20500

Dear President Obama,

Washington State will open 334 marijuana stores and estimates over 2,000 suppliers. The Attorney General's and your administration decision is a slap in the face of every responsible American family. You took an oath to uphold the Constitution and the laws of the land and you are ignoring your duty because you don't want to prosecute them. You want to raise money, instead of always looking for tax increases, put a high fine on illegal marijuana use and use the IRS to collect the funds if the courts can't do it, but enforce the law.

Reid and Boehner declining to meet Russian diplomats regarding Syria would have been a step toward a diplomatic solution. People shouldn't perceive this as a move against the President. The country isn't supporting a military strike against Syria and the NSA have already intercepted threats against our embassies by Iran. There is no such thing as a limited strike in combat. Israel's support for a strike thinks it will have an effect on the nuclear program in Iran also. The European Union Court has decided to lift sanctions against the banks that were supplying funds for the project. Iran has no intention of stopping this program and any future military action should concentrate on that.

Mr. President, standing tall and supporting your convictions at the G20 meeting is admirable, but you must stand tall for the majority of Americans that don't want this conflict. This may hurt your pride if you don't get the support from congress, but it should strengthen your resolve to move forward on immigration, the budget, and the debt limit legislation. Your decision to train the rebels in another country is wiser and will give you an advantage. If you still want to strike, keep it secret, do it when it is advantageous to put the trained rebels over the top and make it the conclusion to the conflict.

Mr. President sometimes we have to walk away from the battle and pick a time when it is better to win the war. A military strike won't guarantee Assad won't use chemical weapons again. A timely strike that will conclude the conflict and remove him will be a better solution.

September 6, 2013

President Barack Obama

1600 Pennsylvania Avenue N.W.

Washington D.C. 20500

Dear President Obama,

Nations are withdrawing their support and waiting for the UN report. It will probably not be as detailed as your intelligence, but it gives them a back door. You are wasting a lot of time on an unpopular resolution. There were millions killed in Africa and the UN and the world did nothing. Assad has killed over 100,000 people and we just woke up because he used a different method. There is no upside to this problem and the nice guy syndrome has to stop. Come home, address the people if you want and back down without the support you need. This is going to turn into a nickel and dime fight and it isn't worth it.

Nancy Pelosi is more worried about the democratic image and will vote yes just to keep face. The majority of America does not want this altercation. Put your efforts and spend your political capital on legislation that is winnable. Believe me, if it gets too hot in the kitchen, Pelosi will be running for takeout.

You are being urged to ease farm work enforcement. Document these workers on the spot if you need to, and help the farmers deliver their products, or the poor people will get hit with the ramifications and high food cost.

Oklahoma and Indiana are exempt from Obamacare until 2015. They have plans that insure the people Obamacare won't cover. I suggest you delay Obamacare and see what they are doing. It may give you ideas that will make Obamacare more desirable. Oklahoma is using the taxes on tobacco to help pay for these people that don't qualify for Medicaid.

I suggest you focus on the fiscal legislation that is coming up and put Syria to the side for now. A decision contrary to American opinion could be disastrous for the democrats in November and you know who will catch hell for that. Democrats are not going to risk going against their constituency. Good luck, no matter what you decide.

September 7, 2013

President Barack Obama

1600 Pennsylvania Avenue N.W.

Washington D.C. 20500

Dear President Obama,

We have an October 1st shutdown deadline to keep the government funded. Since you have telegraphed to the world about a military strike on Syria, you might want to put that on the back burner and make sure our important domestic issues get done first. I know this is an interruption in your agenda, but America does come first.

The congress is only scheduled to work 126 days this year, is there something you can do about that. This is insulting to all hard working Americans. It is more insulting to Americans who don't have jobs. I think Syria can wait.

I noticed, while watching TV and online, the people demonstrating against the strike in Syria are carrying signs that state, jobs not war. Do you think they are trying to send a message? There has not been one definitive bill that has created jobs except getting ready for Obamacare. This has inflated the government ranks over 150,000. I don't know if this is money well spent when part of Obamacare is delayed till next year, Oklahoma and Indiana have been given wavers for one year and congress is working on a bill to delay the personal mandate.

The IRS stated that the personal information gathered is not fully protected because the program is not working correctly, this may be another reason to delay the program. There is a house bill that wants to stop Obamacare because the system to verify house income is not up and running correctly. The program needs to be delayed and fixed.

You will do six TV interviews and a national address on Syria. I has been discovered that part of the products that help Assad accumulate chemical weapons came from America. This is a direct violation of the international agreement. It is bad enough that Russia and Iran are supplying products, but America also. As usual we are supplying weapons to countries we are going to war with. Government sure has a slow learning curve. Do you think it would be smart to include that in the national address?

September 8, 2013

President Barack Obama

1600 Pennsylvania Avenue N.W.

Washington D.C. 20500

Dear President Obama,

Who is talking to Assad from the Whitehouse or are you sending them a message via CBS News? Is the offer for him to get rid of his chemical weapons a viable option? I hope this is the case and it would be the right, the most cost saving and simple solution the problem. I believe you need to put Syria on the back burner for now.

Assad talks about retaliatory strikes if they are attacked. This can come in any form and anywhere, including in the U.S. Reviewing the information sharing on the Boston incident, should give us major concern for any strikes in the U.S. We are not a nation that keeps secrets very well or hire the right people to do it for us.

Congress will go on another recess on September 23, 2013, that gives them 14 days to resolve the funding, debate issues on Obamacare, and the Syrian matter. You have really put yourself in a comer, especially when most of the country is not in favor of the strike on Syria and congress is going home to campaign for reelection. The French people are not in favor of their leaders support for this strike and he has pulled back in favor of the UN Resolution and we know that isn't going to happen.

Countries all over the world are in religious battles. India has Muslins fighting Hindus, there are problems in the Philippines, the fighting continues in Egypt and Iraq and you want to pick a fight in Syria and with the congress before elections. The timing is poor, the issues are complicated and the results can be disastrous.

Who is the big loser in this debacle? Immigration reform will have to take a back seat to Syria, the funding legislation, and resourceful bills that will help Obamacare get off to a better start and possibly be successful. The real problem for you is no one has your back and what little support you get from leadership in congress will fade when the people put their butts on the line. This is a time when you need to count your losses and fold your hand.

September 9, 2013

President Barack Obama

1600 Pennsylvania Avenue N.W.

Washington D. C. 20500

Dear President Obama,

Did you discuss the proposed Russian Plan when you were with Putin or is this a result of your relentless pursuit to attack Syria? If so, what was the point of getting congress and the senate off their game plan when they returned from their needed rest? It is difficult enough for them to function under normal conditions and there you go throwing a monkey wrench into the equation. This looks like the Russians are manipulating you and this is keeping the Obamacare debacle off the front page or is another end run by your administration to distract attention?

I don't understand Israel's support for this attack? The American Israel Public Affairs Group is sending 300 members to congress to push for support of this proposed attack. What would happen if other countries cut off funding our deficit like the congress wants to defund Obamacare? Where does everyone think the money is coming from for these military strikes? I think you should cancel your TV appearance, get congress back on the right track and take care of business at home.

The Heritage group is going to make a substantial push to defund Obamacare. It would be a change of pace if all the organizations that want to stop Obamacare came up with solutions that would make it successful. It would also be a change if you were receptive to delaying the ACA while these group are charged with coming up with solutions for improvement. Their needs to be some innovative thinking in congress, but I don't think they are capable of looking past political affiliations.

What is the point of all this contradiction, is this about not liking you, not liking the way you do things, not liking the lack of transparency you promised, the way you manipulate votes using wavers and showing favoritism, or is it you don't understand the art of compromising? I am not sure myself because your messages are mixed and distracting. I suggest you try a new approach and stay on track and off the TV. It would be a step in the right DIRECTION.

September 10, 2013

President Barack Obama

1600 Pennsylvania Avenue N.W.

Washington D.C. 20500

Dear President Obama,

The Russian Plan to put Syria's chemical weapons under international control is a start. Suspending the vote in congress was your only option. You will still have creditability with our war ship sitting off the coast of Syria. The fact that an army will have to enter Syria to deal with these chemical weapons is not going to sit well with Assad unless Russia tells them, cooperate or no more weapons and military support. Iran might stick it to Russia and provide that support and nothing will be accomplished except good intentions. Russia may have to exercise the threat of force if that happens and I don't think Putin will have to ask for a vote on the matter.

The car bombing in Benghazi was not a spontaneous attack, just as the attack on the embassy was not spontaneous. The cover up was messy, news media coverage of the leaders who planned the attack is insulting to all the agencies involved in bringing the terrorists to justice, and the terrorist's actions demonstrate our weak foreign policy. The complications of the regions sovereignty and the religious fractions creates a no win situation. Unfortunately, military force is the presiding factor over diplomacy.

Your decision not to enforce the federal laws regarding marijuana is creating a fiscal monster in Washington State. Cash only marijuana stores, 334 of them, will surly create criminal activity and an IRS nightmare. This is becoming a nation of pot heads, putting their feel good moments over their responsibilities. This is what you get when it is more important in school about how children feel rather than praising their achievements. I would rather see you honor children's achievements instead of your photo ops with sports teams. Sports recognition should be reserved for our Olympians.

The Detroit bankruptcy is having a major effect on the bond market for municipalities. The city will have to pay a higher rate for their current school bonds and this reduces the capital to help support other programs in the city. There is a great opportunity here with special incentives and private enterprise support beyond the state levels. It can all start with a specific educational program with supported environmental improvements. Think about it.

September 11, 2013

President Barack Obama

1600 Pennsylvania Avenue N.W.

Washington D.C. 20500

Dear President Obama,

　　The Syrian crisis has sent conflicting messages to our allies and our enemies. You have put so many lives in turmoil around the world with a temporary hold on any action. Israel has no choice but to wait and see what you are doing, the Syrian rebels, that were depending on air strikes to help their cause, feel betrayed, and Americans have sent a clear message they don't want another military operation, so the world waits while you and Putin try to come to some agreement on chemical weapons. Does anyone know what Syria thinks about all of this?

　　We are on the road to reestablishing relations with Iran's new President Rouhani, who was educated in America. He has promised his people a better economy and a sure way to achieve that is to do business with America. The American dollar can be the greatest pacifier or the most destructive weapon in the world today if used congruent with all the other major currencies in the world. We need to guard our greatest asset and make wiser choices in its use at home and abroad.

　　The union leadership is calling for a complete delay in Obamacare until it is fixed. It is the sensible thing to do. The unions were built on their ability to secure better health care and retirement benefits for their members and Obamacare, in its present form, is eroding that strength. You have delayed parts of the program, so why should it matter if you delay the entire program for another year, with one exception, maintain the provision for pre-existing conditions. If you can adjust your strategy on war why can't you do it on a domestic matter that will ultimately help all Americans?

　　The recall vote in Colorado is a clear indication that the people are not in charge of this country, but the money backed special interest and lobbying groups are calling the shots. They didn't repeal the new gun law, but they sure got rid of the two politicians who supported stronger background checks by a recall election vote. Political influence in this country is deplorable.

September 12, 2013

President Barack Obama

1600 Pennsylvania Avenue N.W.

Washington D.C. 20500

Dear President Obama,

Al Qaeda is calling for small attacks on the home soil. Zawahri is ordering the sleeper cells to wake up and cause economic calamity in America. Your administration and congress have caused enough economic problems, Zawahri just needs to sit back and wait for the results he wants.

Assad wants the U.S. to stop supplying weapons to the rebels as part of a deal to secure his chemical weapons. Yousef, the rebel commander, claims the rebels have been betrayed and you have lost all your credibility in the world. The Saudis, Brittan and France will continue to supply weapons, but I am sure they will get their notice also. Russia and Syria are playing a game and making us jump through hoops. Kerry is talking about boots on the ground and that is not making anyone happy. So where do you go from here? Whatever you do, be secretive, which is a problem for your administration, make it swift and remove the leadership and Assad at the same time.

The congress will try and use the government shut down against you. They want Obamacare delayed and fixed and frankly, this would be the best option for you. Push back on the pre-existing conditions and get the debt limit raised and a short term budget deal. Bring in the medical experts, insurance experts and drug experts and fix the ACA. Do not allow the lobbyist, just successful working individuals in the industry. Focus on these points to reduce costs and make a reasonable profit for participating companies.

An individual pays directly or indirectly insurance premiums for health care and drug cost to these different companies, medical coverage, drug coverage, workers compensation coverage, thru auto insurance coverage, home insurance coverage, special school insurance coverage and others. Bring all these costs under one coverage, it reduces the profit of these paper companies and will afford better care and reasonable compensation for the people that provide the service, doctor, nurses and hospitals. The coverage has to be nationwide.

It is time to put your politics aside and make deals that will move you closer to making America the greatest country in the world, once again.

September 13, 2013

President Barack Obama

1600 Pennsylvania Avenue N.W.

Washington D.C. 20500

Dear President Obama,

The UN rarely gives us full support on any of our resolutions and the Syrian Resolution is no different. I don't believe they will even support any economic sanctions. You are always dealing with a stacked deck, with Russia and China fixing the cards.

The agreement with Russia instructing Syria to turn over a full list of chemical weapons within a week's time is insulting. A regime that has used these weapons, tortures rebels in the hospitals and goes after doctors that treat the rebels, is going to give us a list of chemical weapons, I don't think so, and the tooth fairy is coming. I think we can do better than this, after all we do have four destroyers sailing off the coast of Syria.

The union leaders came calling and all reports indicate they went home empty handed for now. Get ready for more letters and they won't be from me. This is what you get when you don't treat everyone the same. The wavers and exemptions you approved are coming back to haunt you and will always be a footnote in your legacy. Surprise us all and delay the program until it is fixed and we are all on equal ground.

Social Security has paid 1.3 billion dollars to 36 thousand working people disability benefits. This was over a two year period. Is there a possibility in the next three years of your administration you could put a little more emphasis on waste in government. It seems the right thing to do and it would help the deficit.

How many people beside me need to tell you that Larry Summers is not the right person for the Federal Reserve Job? Four democrats on the senate panel to approve him for the job will vote against him. If they vote with the republicans then he is out, so why waste your time. There are more qualified people who can do the job. Don't waste any political capital on Summers.

September 14, 2013

President Barack Obama
1600 Pennsylvania Avenue N.W.
Washington D.C. 20500

Dear President Obama,

You have warned the republicans, don't oppose raising the debt limit, don't threaten to shut down the government, and don't push for a delay in Obamacare or starve it for money. These are very bold statements when you don't sit in the driver's seat. I wouldn't try to sell the idea of how great the economy is compared to when you started the presidency. The jobless rate and the real jobless numbers are the highest they have ever been. The proof of this is in the number of college graduates who can't find work and the number of people who gave up looking for work.

I suggest the main stabilizer in the economy is the policy of the Federal Reserve, keeping interest rates low and buying bonds. Whenever there was a threat that this would stop or be cut back, the market would drop an average of 500 points. There is no doubt that this will have to slowly come to an end, but you will not help matters by putting Larry Summers in the job. Maybe you can sacrifice him as a bargaining chip to help get what you want.

The gap between the poor and the rich is the widest it has ever been since 1928. All your rhetoric about helping the poor and middle class has produced nothing. The confusion surrounding Obamacare is stalling the job market and aggravating your union friends and you recently rejected their concerns and they represent a good portion of the poor and middle class. Your biggest support group comes from the entitlement population who receive free support and not earned support.

I have seen nothing about educating the poor and middle class in new skills to fill new technical jobs. The job market is becoming highly skilled because of the computers and less workers are needed. Companies are finding out they can get the same production with less workers and that is hurting employment. There needs to be a comprehensive education program for children and adults for them to be competitive.

The bottom line to all of this is you need to compromise and start trading for programs that will help the poor and middle class and the economy. The math is simple, the more people that work, the more taxes you collect and the more you have to spend, not borrow.

September 15, 2013

President Barack Obama

1600 Pennsylvania Avenue N.W.

Washington D.C. 20500

Dear President Obama,

It is good that Larry Summers decided to withdraw his name from consideration for the Federal Reserve job. Your legislative calendar will be challenging enough, worrying about L. Summers confirmation is not what you need now.

Syrian rebels should take the help they are getting and do the best with it. Complaining about what you are doing to help them is not helping you or your support base. The real question over there is who the good guys are and who are the bad guys. We never figured that out in Vietnam and it cost the country dearly.

Iran is training militiamen to help the rebels and we know what side they are on. The entire region is religious driven and that is fractured into different sects. I wonder and I'm sure you and your staff do, who we are really supporting over there and what are they going to be like if they are successful. We do not need another Egypt.

I have heard nothing from Hillary on this matter. The front runner for the 2016 election is being very quiet and not standing in your support line. I guess she isn't sure what will happen, but she will surface when success is close. What exactly did she recommend while Assad was killing his people during her reign as Secretary of State?

I know that it takes time for investigations, but Hillary's 2008 team is being investigated for election irregularities now? She is associated with several investigations with other staff members also. The timing seems a little strange or is it? Will the Benghazi matter ever be resolved or will that surface just before the elections?

I know your life is complicated right now and you need advice from me like you need another bogy, but I consider my common sense advice a lot better than what you are getting right now. Think about it.

September 16, 2013

President Barack Obama

1600 Pennsylvania Avenue N.W.

Washington D.C. 20500

Dear President Obama,

The UN confirmed Syria used chemical weapons against its own people. Russia claims the proof that it was Assad who used the weapons isn't there, which will complicate the deal Kerry made with the Russians. This could turn into a three ring circus real fast and go on forever. Chemical weapons were used, no conclusive evidence who used them, time and advantage has gone by, so find the right rebel group to support and move on with matters in America.

The shooting at the naval base in D.C. is tragic. The people or company that investigate the contractor hired by the government needs to be investigated. Their performance is flawed and the information they provide seems very questionable. Is the government that desperate they have to reduce their standards to find help? It seems that is the direction followed especially in our education standards. We are not only wasting money, we are wasting lives.

The people didn't send you and congress to Washington to complain and blame each other and cause controversy, we sent you there to come up with solutions and solve problems. This is not about who makes the evening news and promoting political parties, everything seems to reflect on how will this affect the election. The government's efficiency rating are pathetic. The people don't pay you and the congress to shut down the government, you are there to keep it functioning efficiently.

The Republicans are trying to reverse the gains of the past five years, what gains are you talking about? Millions of people are still unemployed, more people are dependent on government help, the poor and middle class are sliding backward, and the rich you complain about are getting richer. You are asking congress to raise the debt limit again, Obamacare is not ready to be implemented, and you and congress are in gridlock. Blaming other people does not look good on your resume.

September 17, 2013

President Barack Obama

1600 Pennsylvania Avenue N.W.

Washington D.C. 20500

Dear President Obama,

Gun control, this ghost will follow you forever unless you use a different tactic to resolve the problem. Congress can't solve this problem because their pockets are lined with NRA money. The Constitution guarantees the people the right to own weapons. The government has proven over and over again that they can't solve this problem. The burden belongs on the manufactures and the legal owners.

The government must set standards for the manufactures and the sellers of weapons and provide legislation that will hold them responsible for misuse of documented weapons.

You can't drive a car without training or a license, the same should apply to a weapon, no matter what type of weapon it is.

Investigations should be intensive and include police records, current and past behavior, and have a limited access to mental records.

Weapons should be purchased in person, and in the residing state.

The weapon should have a tracking device built in similar to our cell phones and cars and this device should trigger an alarm if it comes close to a restricted area such as a school.

The weapon should have a recognition system that will allow only the owner to use the weapon.

The manufactures or sellers should set up clubs and ranges that will inspect weapons, recertify training, and have records of intended use.

Ammunition sales should be recorded similar to the method used for prescription drugs and all purchases should match registered weapons.

These are just a few restrictions that can be put on gun owners, sellers and manufactures. Legitimate gun owners should not have any problems with any restrictions placed on them. They should be able to buy any weapon they want as long as the intended use is declared and monitored. Legitimate gun owners need to be a part of making gun ownership more accountable and responsible.

September 18, 2013

President Barack Obama

1600 Pennsylvania Avenue N.W.

Washington D.C. 20500

Dear President Obama,

Would you please remind the bozoes in congress and the senate they were not elected to shut the government down. The spirit of cooperation in Washington sucks and that starts with your administration and permeates through congress and the senate. The system was designed for checks and balance, not to hold the American people hostage while games are being played. You, the congress and the senate are there to come up with solutions, not to suck every dollar you can from the American people and waste it. Delay Obamacare and fix it, raise the debt limit and force congress to come up with better waste controls, not spending cuts, reform the tax code, and start putting America before your political parties. Stop blaming each other and start showing some results and improvements.

Assad stated it will take one year to destroy the chemical weapons and cost one billion dollars. Germany supplies them with the raw materials to make these weapons, let Germany pay the billion dollars and clean up the problem. They helped create the problem, let them fix it.

Maybe the UN can pass a resolution for all countries to stop sending weapons to Syria. Sooner or later they will run out of bombs and bullets and the civil unrest will slow down and a solution may surface. Greed will never let this happen, but who knows, miracles can happen.

Why do they have to pass legislation in the congress that they know will fail in the senate? This is typical government and a waste of time and energy. The supposed leadership and your administration make America politicians look stupid and in some cases they are. What country would want to copy a system that can't get anything done and only works 126 days a year? If all the decisions are made by the leadership and a few members in congress why do we need 435 congress people? Why can't we have 5 congress representatives and one senator from every state, we would reduce the cost of government and more work would get done. No, we can't do that, it makes too much sense.

September 19, 2013

President Barack Obama

1600 Pennsylvania Avenue N.W.

Washington D.C. 20500

Dear President Obama,

I have written you over 300 letters supporting and criticizing your performance as President. It is beyond my comprehension and eludes common sense, why you would go to the Ford Plant, in Kansas City, Missouri, to pitch your message on the economy and blame the GOP for trying to stop the economy from growing. I THINK YOU SHOULD BE TALKING TO CONGRESS AND THE SENATE IN WASHINGTON, PUSHING FOR A RESOLUTION TO THE DEBT LIMIT, BUDGET, AND OBAMACARE. Instead you are going to allow them to waste time with useless votes that the senate or you will veto. Giving the Ford employees a feel good speech is not getting the job done. Blaming the GOP, is not getting the job done. Congress, the Senate and You are at fault for not doing the job you were elected to do.

The President is supposed to lead the country and guide the congress and senate toward sensible legislation for the country, this is not getting done. Last minute solutions produce rushed results and in most cases these results are flawed and there are too many examples of that. You leave yourself open to criticism because of your flawed approach to leadership. The people in your administration are not helping you get your message across to the congress and the senate so it is about time you take the lead and get the job done.

In business, there is a natural flow to problem solving and producing the results. The pros and cons are negotiated and the leader makes the final decision and the plan is carried out. You don't have the final say, but you don't consider the pros and the cons either and this should be done long before the final decision. This is not a my way or the highway agenda, a blame game or let's hope for the best with a last minute compromise. It is a direct reflection on your ability to lead congress, the senate and the country in the right direction and it's not going to happen at the Ford Plant, in Kansas City.

You, congress and the senate owe this country an explanation why the job is not getting done on a timely basis in a spirit of cooperation.

September 20, 2013

President Barack Obama

1600 Pennsylvania Avenue N.W.

Washington D.C. 20500

Dear President Obama,

While you were back slapping at the Ford plant in Kansas City, the congress voted to defund Obamacare. If they had spent as much time fixing the problems as they did voting against it, and you had worked with them instead of pointing blame, the country may have had an ACA that was probable and successful. My take on this is you, congress and the senate wasted time and money on a bill that could have helped all Americans. You are all a failure as a legislative group that could not see the good on either side of the fence. You should all be ashamed of yourselves. Now we are headed for a government shut down because, for over three years, you and congress sniped at each other instead of fixing an important piece of legislation. Dummies!

Your support for the contraceptive mandate is flawed. The drug should be made available and free at all medical facilities and drug stores for certain age individuals. You mucked up this portion of the ACA when you intruded on religious rights and made it an employer mandate. If the availability of these drugs will reduce the amount of abortions in this country, then it should be free. Naturally, regulations and restrictions should be put on them so it doesn't turn into a black market drug. At least it will be the choice of the individual and not interfere with religious beliefs.

I have never been a supporter of government involvement in individual's lives, but when I see the country and the world going GAGA over an I Phone, it makes me wonder if we do need some regulation over our personal behavior. Maybe Apple needs to create a better way of selling their new products or just sell them online so it doesn't create problems for other people. What people did to the homeless in Los Angelis is shameful just so they could get an I Phone.

NATO is concerned about the training of the Afghan Air Force after we leave in 2014. Why are we wasting money on an air force for a country that can't feed its people? What is the point of supplying weapons to countries that don't respect us or want to cooperate with us unless there is a dollar in it for them? An Afghan Air Force, is this a joke?

September 21, 2013

President Barack Obama

1600 Pennsylvania Avenue N.W.

Washington D.C. 20500

Dear President Obama,

After over 300 letters, with many criticisms and few accolades, I have decided to share your letters with Senator Harry Reid and Congressman John Boehner, who I consider just as and even more responsible, for the dismal performance and infighting in the government. I hope their staff will respond as often as your staff has with pertinent explanations of their behavior in the congress and the senate. Their leadership styles have convoluted some of your good ideas and failed to prevent some of your misguided legislation. That said, all three of you need to learn the spirit of cooperation, consideration and compromise to bring America back to a great economy and respected world power, where hard work, perseverance and common sense have been the driving force for our success in the past.

Why are you scheduled to travel across the country and push Obamacare when the government is faced with a shutdown? The tripod needs to resolve the current problems, and stop throwing the piss pot at each other. There is more at stake than the three of you and your personal agendas.

There is no decision on how many troops will be left behind in Afghanistan at the end of this year. Is this going to be another last minute decision? I think they should all come home and let that country decide their own fate. They have survived long before Russia or the U.S. ever went there and they will continue to survive.

Mr. President, I'm not sure if you can do this, but why don't you suspend weapon sales in the U.S. until the government comes up with a viable solution. I have sent you my thoughts on this several times and it seems to me more people are dying from gun violence than from terroristic events in this country. I have always maintained that government should set the standards and the manufactures and sellers should be responsible to enforce the standards. The least you can do is demand that tracking devices and palm grips be installed on all weapons that will trigger an alarm on equipped public events and places such as schools. This will definitely help prevent future assaults in public places. Maybe an executive order?

The American taxpayer deserves better performance from the Congress, the Senate and you for the pay and benefits you are paid. I suggest we establish a civilian review board that will monitor the criminal behavior and performance of the Senate and Congress.

September 22, 2013

President Barack Obama

1600 Pennsylvania Avenue N.W.

Washington D.C. 20500

Dear President Obama,

It is time for you to go face to face with the congress and senate, especially with Cruz and Paul and explain the facts of life to them. No matter what the politicians want Obamacare is here to stay or fail. The vote by congress was just another delay. Over the last three years neither party sought to improve the flawed legislation and neither did you Mr. President. You all look foolish granting wavers, delaying portions of the bill and never reacting to the people's and legitimate business concerns.

The poor leadership from Reid and Boehner is another example of the time wasted while people are killed in the streets every day. They are just as responsible as the shooter for putting politics over the lives of the American people. The Obamacare issue should have been settled two years ago and we should have moved forward as one nation not the fractured mess you and the President created. When are you going to start doing the job you were elected to do?

The Supreme Court will hear a case involving personal donations to political parties and individual politicians. The politicians want no limits on the donations and the people want limits. The decision by the Supreme Court to allow companies to donate as much as they want was stupid. This allowed uncontrollable political influence. Going around the barn to give money to PAC's is another joke. The argument is the individual vote has no influence on election results. The results follow the money in most cases. The Supreme Court slapped every American in the face with their last decision. I hope they have enough brains to make the right decision this time.

Mr. President, tell La Pierre of the NRA, that manufactures and sellers of weapons will be held responsible for the weapons they sell and if they are used in a crime and traced back to the seller and manufacture, they can be sued. The NRA must stop asking the government to fix a problem they created and they profit from. Make it a part of the sale of the weapon that they submit to a psychiatric examine and background investigation at their own expense with the results decided on by the seller or manufacture. They want the profit, make them responsible.

September 23, 2013

President Barack Obama

1600 Pennsylvania Avenue N.W.

Washington D.C. 20500

Dear President Obama,

Reelection politics play a bigger role in legislation over the constructive and reasonable solutions. This is a clear indication why term limits should exist. All senate and congressional representatives should serve one term, four years for the house and six years for the senate. Too much time is spent on reelections and not enough time on constructive legislation. The work schedule for congress and the senate should resemble the schedule the everyday American has to follow, not 126 day session currently being followed. They can get more done if they are in Washington and not running around their state trying to get reelected.

Lois Lerner retired from the IRS, are you going to give her a party or will you call for a continued investigation in her treatment of the American taxpayers and nonprofit organizations?

Insurance companies are sending out false information in order to keep their healthy customers. One company has been fined at the state level and others are under investigation. You have created a monster with Obamascare and I wonder will you be covered by this plan when you retire or are you exempt like the rest of the politicians in Washington? You blast the rich about their wealth, and you made them wealthier, and you created a special class of people by not insisting the politicians and the government staff be covered by Obamacare, which alone should have derailed the program. Your trademark legislation makes it very clear where the average American stands versus the rich and the politicians in this country. So much for equal rights!

Another fine example of government efficiency, the government hires a firm to investigate people for high security clearance jobs and they missed Alexis's shooting incidents. Twelve people die and we have a legislature that can't pass a sensible gun control bill. Maybe if they worked more than 126 days a year and they would do a better job.

Dog Track Harry is going to hold the CR bill off till Sunday giving politicians a whole day to resolve the problem and this is the treatment the American people deserve, politics over accomplishments. Other than your veto, what other constructive solutions do you have for the CR bill before Sunday?

September 24, 2013

President Barack Obama

1600 Pennsylvania Avenue N.W.

Washington D.C. 20500

Dear President Obama,

Obamacare has been contracted out to private agencies to do what the government can't do itself. Federal prosecutors have convicted over 350 government employees and private contractors for falsified information on background checks for security clearance, what do you think is going to happen when there is no income verification in place for the exchanges for Obamacare? After spending money for advertising, navigators, and private contractors, what is going to be left for the medical professionals who have to treat the patients? This entire process, from start to implementation, is a bureaucratic nightmare that will continue.

Mr. President, Harry Reid and John Boehner have delivered a slow fused economical bomb to the American people that will set our economy back again. My father told me you can't give something to the people that you don't take from someone else. Well, we have taken from the social security fund, we borrowed from China and Japan, we are trying to take from the rich that are becoming richer and we are 17 trillion in the hole, so where is the money going to come from to fund Obamacare? We currently spend 524 billion on Medicare and 302 billion on Medicaid, and we are giving tax credits for Obamacare in a slow economy with poor employment prospects. Delay and fix Obamacare.

Mr. President, your goal to establish a Palestinian State and easing the confrontational diplomacy with Iran is admirable but shortsighted. They only like our money and they are not going to stop their nuclear program, but in this case talk will be good but cheap. You will never solve the religious difference between these nations in the Middle East and you are sending mixed messages to Israel. Focus your time on getting our troops home and creating jobs for them when they get here. That is more important.

It has been noted in a New York Times article how we are ready to sign an Arms Treaty with other countries that will put restrictions on the weapons industry in America, but we can't come up with significant gun control laws in our own country.

Ted Cruz has been talking all day and night about Obamacare and you and Clinton were talking during the day and neither demonstrates the leadership that Obamacare needs to make it successful. Good intentions being smothered by egotistical politicians.

September 25, 2013

President Barack Obama

1600 Pennsylvania Avenue N.W.

Washington D.C. 20500

Dear President Obama,

The senate voted to vote on the CR bill after listening to Cruz for 20 plus hours. They actually voted to do the job they are being paid for, amazing. Cruz spent all that time telling the American people what is wrong with the ACA and not one minute on how to resolve the problems. I guess those Harvard Degrees floating around Washington focused on debates more than they focused on results and negotiations.

The IRS can't account for 67 million dollars of a 488 million dollar fund set up for the implementation of Obamacare, from 2010 to2012, according to the Treasury Inspector General for Taxes. Another 360 million is set aside for 2013 and 440 million set aside for 2014, this is over a billion dollars to implement the ACA that is ripe with technical problems, wavers and partial delays. At the current rate of undocumented spending, 176 million dollars will go unaccounted for. The IRS stated they have put corrective measures in place. Good luck with that.

The Post Master wants a three cent increase in stamps. This is a great way for you to collect money without raising taxes. If they don't get the increase and other measures of cost cutting, they will have a six billion dollar loss. This will cost the businesses more money, which will get passed down to the poor and middle class in product increases. To offset this cost, they can make a call rather than sending Christmas cards. This will make the environmentalist happy because we won't have to cut down more trees. Give them the three cent increase.

The UAW and the National Labor Relations Board are at odds over the cards that were signed at the Volkswagen plant in West Virginia and Tennessee. Employees claimed they were misled about the meaning of the cards and filed complaints with the NLRB. The UAW stated they could have their cards back, which indicated they supported the UAW and are considered a vote for the union. I hope the NLRB makes the right decision and does a thorough investigation.

I mentioned sometime ago about the burden you were putting on the medical professionals and the lack of a program to help supplement the industry faced with new and aging patients every day. The board you put together to deal with this problem was never funded as part of the law and has never meant. I haven't seen anything written about it to indicate that is being addressed. I hope the quality of care doesn't erode because of the influx of new patients for an overworked and short staffed medical industry.

September 26, 2013

President Barack Obama

1600 Pennsylvania Avenue N.W.

Washington D.C. 20500

Dear President Obama,

What a mess the politicians have created in this country because they can't determine what the difference is in common sense versus political sense. Arguing over the ACA is a waste of time. Since congress won't fix it and you won't delay it for a year so it can be fixed, stand your ground and let it take its own course. The problem with this is congress won't fix any of the problems that surface as the bill is implemented. This is like to jackasses, hitched up in different directions to the same wagon, trying to pull it. It is never going to happen.

The solution is simple, have a medical industry panel resolve the problems within the CPI and pass it on to the IRS which has the regulatory power to change the program. Have congress pass a law to allow insurance companies to sell nationwide with national coverage. Negotiate what you have to and make this happen so the ACA will be successful. It will never be successful as long as congress holds the purse strings. Let the free market regulate it and make it successful. Everyone must contribute something to the plan even if it is only $10.00 a month, and everyone should be on the plan including you, the senate, congress and all federal employees. I would be happy to lead this panel to a positive solution. IT CAN BE DONE.

It is ironic that the original ACA plan came from the Heritage Foundation, a think tank for the republicans, and they have not come up with solutions to the problems of their own plan. This is more about you and the way you rammed the plan through congress and changed the penalty to a tax. Putting new taxes in the plan that have nothing to do with health care didn't help. This is a genius nation fighting against its own intelligence, truly amazing.

Before you spend a dime in Detroit, demand that the government and the courts fix their pension problem first or it will be a waste of money. This is like buying a used car, you will have to nickel and dime it to keep it going. Resolve their issues and then invest the money.

The state conservatives and any politician that is against making it illegal to sell child porn and traffic in child sex online should go directly to jail and not pass go. There is no argument for freedom of rights that should ever supersede this grievous criminal activity. I would even suspend search and seizure laws regarding this activity. The Constitution did not intend to condone freedom for this activity, speech or otherwise. Revolting.

September 27, 2013

President Barack Obama

1600 Pennsylvania Avenue N.W.

Washington D.C. 20500

Dear President Obama,

You can talk to Iran but you won't talk with the republicans or extremists, as you refer to them. In case you missed this, they were elected by people that don't agree with you. The reason they control the congress is because lots of people don't agree with you. You have a lot of nerve condemning them for doing what their constituents want. A 43% approval rating means you have some room for improvement.

Telling college students to go and apply for Obamacare when they are covered under a family policy and have student loans is a little counterproductive. How can you suggest to anyone to do something you, congress and the senate won't do yourself? How can you exempt some people, but tell everyone else they have to apply for Obamacare or they will be fined? Forget all the problems with the program, if it is good for one than it should be good for all, but that isn't the case and you wonder why people don't want to support Obamacare.

The people who will sign up for Obamacare are the people that need help and that is good and the people that think they will get something for nothing. When they find out it will cost them something they will disappear, because they know they can walk into any ER and be treated.

I am tired of your lack of attention to details, delaying parts of the program that need your attention, spreading confusion and disparity throughout America, blaming everyone except yourself, and condoning the waste that has already surfaced and the program hasn't started. You rammed this ACA through the house and senate and you lost the house as a result and now you are blaming them even though they have suggested alternatives. Where are your alternatives?

The ACA starts on October 1st no matter what. Are they going to have the necessary funding to move forward or will they have to wait until you and congress stop playing games? This should have all been done and decided before they went on recess. Now we are into more short term deals that will solve nothing. It is time for you to be the President and realize that you are 1/4th of the equation, then we have the senate, congress and the people that put them there, you keep forgetting them.

September 28, 2013

Dear President Obama,

The house passed the bill to delay Obamacare and approved funding till December 15th. The senate will make their move and nothing will be resolved until all three sides come together and compromise on a solution. You are abusing the people that put you into office to do a job and you have all failed. None of you have shown the leadership required to break this impasse and the American people will be the big losers.

According to the NY Times, there are major flaws in the mental health sections of the ACA. Patrick Kennedy blames it on your givebacks to the insurance companies for their support of the ACA in 2010. Your administration is dragging their feet on these changes. In lite of the fact that mental health is a key reason for gun violence in this country, don't you think it is important enough for you to kick your administration in the butt and give the insurance companies the clarification they need to pay for authorized and needed treatment? Did you really COMPROMISE with the insurance companies as Kennedy claims?

The Highway Transportation Fund is out of money and the CBO recommended to raise the gas tax 10 cents and index it on a yearly basis to the rate of inflation. I think this recommendation should be tied to research and construction that will make the roads last longer. I really object to giving California 3.5 billion a year which is almost 10% of the 40 billion dollar fund. I understand they have more people and pay more taxes, but I think they should take on more of their own responsibility even though they are a democratic state that helped put you in the Whitehouse.

Kansas, Oklahoma and several other states are cutting back on food stamps for able single adults, under 49 years old that can work. Congress is trying to pass a similar bill for the nation. The law makes sense and can stop the beach bums in California from eating Lobster at a barbeque.

What are the copays associated with Obamacare? I don't see them mentioned anywhere and I know that was a problem in Massachusetts for the poor that couldn't afford them or the insurance.

September 29, 2013

President Barack Obama

1600 Pennsylvania Avenue N.W.

Washington D.C. 20500

Dear President Obama,

    Serving the people can be a thankless, time consuming, family destroying job, but you, Boehner, and Reid asked for it and you got it. During this impending crisis, it is apparent that there has been no communication between the leadership except to blame each other in the media. Is this what you were elected to do? You, Reid, and Boehner, the media, and the people have been arguing over Obamacare for three years and not one change has been made to correct the discrepancies or put together a panel that could offer solutions. Deplorable behavior by all.

    Holder's law suit over voters rights face a tough challenge. He has to prove the states are keeping people away from the voter box, which is not the case. The real issue here is if you really want to vote then you should do whatever it takes to get registered. For example, it is more difficult to get a driver's license in New Jersey than it is to register to vote. It is all about your personal priorities and some people could care less about voting. There is nothing in the law that states you have to vote, just the right to vote. Personally, I think a one day window to vote in person is restrictive, but that is the rule we have to live with so people make arrangements to see it happen. The only thing that stops a person from voting is their own conviction.

    Mr. President, I want you to know that some of the people that read my letters to you are intelligent, inquisitive, concerned, offer constructive criticism, are very supportive of you, and some are downright nasty. I can deal with all of this because I communicate with concerned Americans wither they agree with me or not and some have made considerable arguments. What bothers me the most, is their legitimate concern and communication doesn't translate to the leadership of this nation. I am sure outside this group, there are many Americans communicating and offering solutions to the current problems. Why aren't you, Reid and Boehner doing the same thing? The nation needs all of you to get over your petty differences and insults and get the job done.

September 30, 2013

President Barack Obama

1600 Pennsylvania Avenue N.W.

Washington D.C. 20500

Dear President Obama,

The government is shutting down because you and congress think you both have the people on your side, and the only loser here is the American people. You and congress have doomed this law to failure by your deceit, and public manipulation. There have been more lies or misrepresentations about the ACA that have caused the hard lines and a shutdown.

Companies are canceling insurance coverage, so people may not have the same doctor or an insurance policy at all.

The unions and other companies are getting wavers and exemptions. The ACA is the law of the land, what gives you the right to apply the law in different direction?

Two states are exempt from the law for one year. Why can't the other 48 states have the same exemption?

The Medicaid portion of the bill supporting poor people has less than 50% participation and will reduce or eliminate coverage for the poor.

There are 51 new taxes in the bill that the people will have to pay directly or indirectly. Why is there a real estate tax in the health care bill?

The 30 hour work week requirement has given businesses a back door for backing out of coverage and reversed the hiring of full time employees.

The information technology is flawed and there isn't a definitive way to verify people's income requirements. The plan makes people buy more expensive insurance than they currently have.

The list goes on and the waste and fraud will follow the ACA just like it does in Medicare. There are more than enough reason to delay the ACA and prevent a shutdown of the government, but that is not what this is all about.

You talked about congress being responsible and doing their job, what about your job. You, congress and the senate are all vying for the tough kid on the block award, when the reality is you are all a feckless bunch of kids all wanting the same lollypop. Despicable, all of you.

October 1, 2013

President Barack Obama

1600 Pennsylvania Avenue N.W.

Washington D.C. 20500

Dear President Obama,

There is a simple solution to the ACA and shutdown crisis. Establish a national referendum and put the ACA on the ballot in November. Let the people decide if they want the ACA to continue in force. I know it is already a law and an unpopular law. Make it clear in the referendum that it cannot be reversed by legislation even if one party holds all three branches of government. Establish a max on spending and tie all increases to the CPI. Have everyone participate, no exemption or wavers and establish a minimum payment for everyone. People that don't want the insurance will have to pay double premiums after ten years of no insurance and triple premiums after another ten years of no insurance. Make the insurance national coverage with companies allowed to sell in every state, no picking and choosing. Establish a high risk pool and distribute the risks proportionally.

These are suggestions and more can be added to the referendum, all in plain language. This legislation should not be held hostage and should have never been passed by congress with the 80 congressmen that were leaving office. The process that was followed has caused this crisis and it will get worse when the debt limit legislation comes in play. This is legislation where the people should have the last word, not the politicians.

Blaming each other is not accomplishing anything and causing congress to finagle legislation to point blame. It is clear that this could go on for a long time and the people will be the big losers in the end. You, congress and the senate were not elected to play a game of chicken.

A note to all you hard ass objectors to health care for everyone, your money and your attitude about having to pay someone else's medical bill won't help you if you're sick. It is the total participation by everyone, especially on the preventive side of medical care that will help reduce cost and treatments and help find the cures for uncontrollable diseases. For all you people who schlep through life and think you are owed medical care and avoid your personal responsibilities to stay healthy, you are the primary objection to medical care for everyone. You cheat the poor and disadvantaged that require lagitament medical help. This is an all for one and one for all situation, it is too bad the politicians don't see that.

October 2, 2013

President Barack Obama

1600 Pennsylvania Avenue N.W.

Washington D.C. 20500

Dear President Obama,

Straight talk, the ACA bill you signed and never read is leaving millions of the poorest people without insurance through Medicaid and the ACA, this according to a front page New York Times article. The article is supported by the fact that some states did not expand the Medicaid program and the ACA did not make provision for this. The people who need the coverage the most have been left out in the cold again because you, Dog Track Harry and Queen Pelosi rushed the bill to passage.

You need to use a delay of the bill, a fix of the bill and national coverage of the bill to make a deal and stop the shutdown of government, the CR bill and the debt ceiling bill. You basically have left poor Americans out on a battlefield with no help in sight. The ACA was supposed to help the weakest first and you used them and discarded them. Now is the time to negotiate a new deal that will benefit every American equally.

Congress and the senate have to pass a CR bill for services promised to the people, but keep the government shut down till you all come to an agreement on the ACA. This is possible with the bills that congress is moving forward on the individual mandates.

There is no equitable foundation in the ACA with the exemptions, wavers and state exemptions. The most important part of the bill is that everyone must have health insurance, supported by the Supreme Court, has not provided the provisions to do that. Strip the bill and use the Medicare program as a model and use funding models from congress, the senate, the insurance industry, the hospital conglomerates and the five best business schools in the country. Seek the advice of doctors, nurses, medical billing agencies and the people and get the job done right.

This is a moment to show courage and trust from you, the congress and the senate. I suggested a civilian panel before to help maneuver the ACA to a successful and practical resolution. The time is now and the time is right.

October 3, 2013

President Barack Obama

1600 Pennsylvania Avenue N.W.

Washington D.C. 20500

Dear President Obama,

Why aren't you insisting that the CR Bill be in Conference Committee? This is the next step when the congress and the senate can't agree on a major bill. At least the committee would be talking while you, the congress and the senate are playing your game. You had three years to present legislation to correct some of the problems with the ACA and you neglected to do it. You have forced congress to take this action because of major flaws in the ACA so you are as much the blame as they are. If you are pulling Reid's strings, then pull the one that will start the conference process.

Going through this calamity over the ACA that isn't doing what it was intended to do is a slap in the face to all Americans especially the people that are out of work and the people that won't be covered by the program. I can't believe that you actually read the bill or had an intelligent staff review it and point out the pitfalls and the strong attributes of the bill. Your decisions to exempt and delay portions of the bill does not demonstrate equality and democracy. A bill that is passed by the congress and the senate should not be altered by one person and the rules should not be altered to accommodate different groups in the population. The implementation of this controversial law has caused direct grief and misfortune to America.

You, the congress and the senate should pass a clean CR and Debt Ceiling Bill and let the ACA move towards its own destruction in its present form. The major contributor to this is the government's lack of control in fiscal matters especially the waste of money spent on two wars that produced nothing but more controversy and long term debt. We have an obligation to pay our debts and we should, but we should also figure a way to control ourselves and our fiscal matters.

This game of stupidity has stopped other important legislation and medical treatment for children and veterans. It has added to our foolish image around the world and I am sure our enemies are pointing out the pitfalls of our democracy.

October 4, 2013

President Barack Obama

1600 Pennsylvania Avenue N.W.

Washington D.C. 20500

Dear President Obama,

You sold the democrats and America on the ACA because it would provide coverage for everyone. This is a misrepresentation, it does not provide coverage for everyone. You and Reid are adamant about not discussing the ACA during conference for the CR bill and the house wants to discuss it. They claim there are problems that need to be fixed and they are right.

When the Supreme Court found the individual fine, which you later claimed was a tax, constitutional, they gave the states the right to opt out of the Medicaid portion of the law and many did. This put the poorest in our nation without coverage in the Medicaid program and the ACA. People that made too much income for Medicaid did not make enough money for subsidies or tax credits under the ACA. This left them with no affordable coverage. People that are here on green cards are not eligible for Medicaid for five years, but are eligible for subsidies or tax credits under the ACA depending on their income and family status.

The GOP wants to discuss the medical tax, maybe you should suggest to discuss Americans without coverage first as a starting point and how the states that can't afford to expand Medicaid can be helped so that all Americans can get health care coverage of some kind. There are numerous problems with the ACA that can be discussed as a starting point for negotiations, so why don't you pick one and start talking. Tell Reid, I am sure the children that are waiting for cancer treatment would also appreciate conference negotiations.

You and congress have created a real mess for the hard working Americans. The federal employees will probably get back pay as they usually do, but the rest of the Americans who are not working because of the shutdown will not get back pay. They will suffer the adverse effects of this inexcusable performance and behavior by the leadership in this country. Why the American people take sides and support the efforts of the leadership in this country is beyond my understanding. You, Reid and Boehner should all be subject to a recall election, but we can't do that with the government shutdown.

October 5, 2013

President Barack Obama

1600 Pennsylvania Avenue N.W.

Washington D.C. 20500

Dear President Obama,

The shut down and the impending debt ceiling legislation is making our political system look like the amateur hour, here and around the world. We are fighting over a law that was passed three years ago and have done nothing in the interim to fix the problems that surfaced before its implementation. Quite frankly, no one really knows or agrees with what results the law will produce. There isn't a federal agency or political party that can accurately predict what will happen as the ACA progresses. The time is here to put this argument aside and let the law stand on its merits or failures. The people will decide that after they experience the actual operation of the law. The insurance company's execution of the law will be the nail in the coffin or the icing on the cake. IT IS TIME FOR THE HOUSE TO TAKE IT OFF THE TABLE AND AGRUE THE MERITS OF THE CR AND DEBT CEILING LEGISLATION ON THEIR OWN.

Mr. President, stop negotiating with Afghanistan. It is time to bring all the troops home. That country survived for thousands of years before Russia and the U.S. were there and they will continue to survive on their own. Stop any monetary support except humanitarian support that we control and provide. We are a giving nation, but we don't have to give to their politicians, we give too much to our own.

Khamenei of Iran doesn't trust you or the U.S. and they are buying time to press their own agenda. They are hoping that you will lift some of the sanctions that are in place. North Korea sang the same song and Clinton caved and we got a kick in the butt. Iran's hand is out but they are not holding palm, so don't be fooled by this gesture. The simple fact is they don't like America.

It is nice that the law was passed to pay the federal employees back pay for the shutdown. What about all the other people that lost paychecks because you and congress wanted to play chicken. You are all the blame for this. This was not a surprise to any of you and no one did anything to head it off. This is a blatant waste of time and money and nothing good will come out of it.

What do you think will happen when tax time rolls around in 2015 and some people might have to pay part of the subsidies back provided for by the ACA? Do you really think people will budget for this possibility? Could this be the nail in the coffin?

October 6, 2013

President Barack Obama

1600 Pennsylvania Avenue N.W.

Washington D.C. 20500

Dear President Obama,

You, Reid, Pelosi, Boehner and McConnell took the oath of office and pledged to uphold and defend the Constitution of the United States of America. You were elected by Americans that gave you the authority to conduct the business and legislation of our country.

YOU WERE NOT GIVEN THE AUTHORITY TO CONDUCT BUSINESS OR LEGISLATION FOR THE DEMOCRATIC OR REPUBLICAN PARTY.

YOU WERE NOT GIVEN THE AUTHORITY TO CONDUCT BUSINESS OR LEGISLATION FOR THE KOCH BROTHERS OR GEORGE SOROS.

YOU WERE NOT GIVEN AUTHORITY TO DEFAULT ON OUR FISCAL OBLIGATIONS, DENY CHILDREN MEDICAL TREATMENT, PUT PEOPLE OUT OF WORK AND FRACTURE THE COOPERATION AND SPIRIT OF AMERICA.

YOUR DISREGARD FOR THE CONSTITUTION AND THE PEOPLE OF THE UNITED STATES OF AMERICA DICTATES ONE CONCLUSION, GET THE JOB DONE OR ALL OF YOU RESIGN.

October 7, 2013

President Barack Obama

1600 Pennsylvania Avenue N.W.

Washington D.C. 20500

Dear President Obama,

You called out Boehner, now it is time for him to put up or shut up. I can't believe that no one in the House is call for the same vote. These representatives were not elected to cow down to Boehner. This is an insult to the American people, especially the people directly suffering from this display of nonsense.

Mr. President, what are you going to do if they vote against you? Reid is working on the senate version of the bill and calling for a vote on Friday, this is a joke, right. Voting on Friday puts the House in a corner. If the senate voted earlier, don't you think that might have a positive influence on the House, unless naturally, they voted on party lines? This process could possibly produce another show down, then what do we do start all over again?

Three years we had to configure the online exchanges and look what we have, confusion and breakdown of the system. We can send a Rover to Mars, but we can't implement a law that is basically, fill in the blanks. Your administration supplied the ammunition to the GOP with this lack luster attempt of administering the ACA. A smooth rollout would have taken the wind out of their sails, but they are moving along with the jet stream on this one. The repair process doesn't seem to be improving the condition. I know we can blame it on the volume, but the NSA doesn't seem to have a problem with the volume of information they gather. Maybe they should have designed the program for you.

The left or progressives are angry about you spying on them. Tell them to get over it. I commend you for standing your ground and putting the security of the country over a bunch of hypocrites. Once you put your information out online you give up your privacy right to any hacker here or abroad that wants that information. There is nothing secret about our lives anymore and the agencies we trust with our information are doing a poor job of protecting it. So, whatever measures you need to take to keep our country safe, do it. Maybe they should try to mail letters more often, it still seems to be the safer way to transmit information.

October 8, 2013

President Barack Obama

1600 Pennsylvania Avenue N.W.

Washington D.C. 20500

Dear President Obama,

The ACA state exchanges are having better results than the federal exchanges. Why is that not a surprise? They are simpler to operate and don't require you to have an account just to look at your options for insurance, which makes a lot of sense to me. Why overload the system with information if the person is a looker and not a buyer? Is there other possible motivation for this requirement?

Writing about the shutdown these days is like asking what you are going to have for breakfast. Action is what is needed, not just verbiage. Have the House send you a letter of what they want. You check off what you are willing to discuss and cross out what you won't discuss. Discussing nothing is not going to get the job done, since that is your point of negotiation, don't send them a letter, wait for theirs. The point, do something besides criticizing each other.

The Supreme Court is hearing a case on donation limits for political parties. How about this limit, ZERO. This would apply to state and local elections also. The states could set up a limited number of public, televised debates for its citizens, with reruns for the people that missed it. This would not give the parties a financial edge and people would have to make decisions on the candidates and not the walking around money and donations. This would not eliminate the handsome or pretty factor, but might enhance the intelligent factor. This should also apply to corporate donations. They should also include PACS since you can never figure who is lying and who is telling the truth. Wishful thinking, I know.

Why are open air national monuments being closed? Why are some people allowed to demonstrate at some monuments and not others? Is free speech and expression only reserved for the National Mall? This is silly. The greatest nation in the world is shut down because politicians who we pay to talk won't talk. You can't get them to shut up when it is election time, but they won't do their job either, that includes you Mr. President. The people need you to start a constructive dialog not destructive criticism.

October 9, 2013

President Barack Obama

1600 Pennsylvania Avenue N.W.

Washington D.C. 20500

Dear President Obama,

Sometimes protocol needs to be put aside and face to face conversations need to take place. Inviting the republicans to the Whitehouse isn't the answer. Talking to all of them at the same time is like talking to Boehner alone. He does not have the guts to keep his House in order or know when to pick the right battles. The problem with a face to face conversation is you have nothing to offer but spending cuts. It is clear from the roll out of the ACA you will need support from the House and Senate to fix some of the problems it has and has created. You must consider that and cut some deals with your adversaries.

Reid and Boehner are like two old men fighting over an old girlfriend. Their vision is blurred and Reid's advice to you and your administration is no better than getting a tip at the race track. All this bickering back and forth is going to produce another short term deal. The world's greatest nation can't operate more than two months at a time. This signals a great investment opportunity for foreign investment. As for the Tea Party, give them some good advice if you meet with them, they can't fix all the problems by themselves and if this is their only method of negotiating, they will go the way of the Ford's Edsel. They are creating more problems than they are solving.

Russia will help Vietnam build a nuclear power plant starting in 2014 and Japan will help them in 2025. Kerry has signed a treaty to supply information and technology to Vietnam. Where do you think this is going to go twenty years from now? The Russians and Japanese didn't learn their lessons and it seems like we haven't learned ours. Before you send this treaty to congress, I suggest you find out if there are other alternatives for power plants in Vietnam. Sharing our technology with the world has done nothing but create more world problems.

I know that Nelson Mandela stated that education is a powerful weapon that can help change the world, but it doesn't seem to be working here. I think it is time to add some common sense to that equation and that seem to be in short supply in Washington, D.C.

October 10, 2013

President Barack Obama

1600 Pennsylvania Avenue N.W.

Washington D.C. 20500

Dear President Obama,

Paul Ryan's plan has started some progress in the fiscal talks. Where is Harry Reid plan? Where is John Boehner's plan? Where is your plan? Why couldn't this invitation have been extended 10 days ago or a month ago? You, Reid and Boehner have put America's back up against the wall, have caused grievous aggravation and emotional distress to many Americans, and have created a fiscal mess in family budgets that spend within their means. Now there seems to be a glimmer of hope for a resolution so don't mess it up.

Obamacare is off to a bumpy start and that is no surprise. Over a billion dollar has been spent preparing for the roll out of Obamacare and it is a train wreck. The state run programs are doing much better and signing up more people than the government program. It would have been simpler and cheaper if the designated insurance companies operated their own market place. The problem with that is it wouldn't give the government all the information gathering legally, not that they need any legal grounds these days to collect information. You should have started the program like you rationed gas in the tough times, even number birthdates apply on even numbered days and odd number birthdates apply on odd numbered days. This would have stopped the system from massive overload. It can still be done, think about it.

I think it is time for the House and the Senate to elect new leaders. The American people deserve to know who is in charge and who are the motivating forces in the different parties. They also need a clear picture of the party's goals and objectives and where they all stand on the spending and health care issues that brought this fiscal mess upon the American people. It is very difficult to believe that a few congressmen were able to create this impasse and if that is the case then the system isn't working. Your," I will not negotiate," posture sucks. That is why you were elected to represent the American people and negotiate their future and best interest.

October 11, 2013

President Barack Obama

1600 Pennsylvania Avenue N.W.

Washington D.C. 20500

Dear President Obama,

Essential government workers are working without paychecks. They have expenses and costs just to get them to work besides feeding their families and paying their bills. The people that are working deserve to be paid. How do you think they will feel when the other workers return that did not work and they are being paid to stay home? Then there are the workers that are associated with the government that will not get paid at all. Government workers that are not working should not be paid. You and congress did not do your job, so many Americans have to suffer so you all can play politics. The entire congress should face recall election if the budget isn't passed on time. If the President vetoes the budget and it isn't passed on time, the President should be recalled. You are all an embarrassment to America.

The Free Syrian Army is short on Ammunition and supplies they were promised. The rebels are splitting up and going over to the extreme factions that have ammunition and supplies. Even if they manage to remove Assad they will be fighting, with each other forever, just as they have done for years. It doesn't take a brain surgeon to figure where the extremist support is coming from.

Iran is buying time just like North Korea did and stuck it to us down the road. You are leaving Israel and Turkey hanging out in the wind while you play nice with a country that hates America. What part of that don't you understand? Iran claims they have an excess of 20% enriched uranium they want to get rid of. I wonder what that is all about, a country that wants a nuclear bomb getting rid of enriched uranium.

Afghanistan wants us out and the military wants a base to run operations from. The Afghanistan want us to give them our intelligence and they will run the operations. What is wrong with this picture? They can't defend themselves and they want to run operation across the border. This will be another army we are supplying and will use the weapons against us in the future. Take the troops and leave them to their own devices. We spilled enough blood there for an ungrateful country.

The outside money is pouring into the Virginia governor's race. Sixty six percent of the republican donations and seventy four present of the democratic donations are coming from outside sources. Is this a government by the people or by the dollar?

October 12, 2013

President Barack Obama
1600 Pennsylvania Avenue N.W.
Washington D.C. 20500

Dear President Obama,

If all you need is a piece of paper stating that we can pay our bills, you have my permission to pay our bills and you have my permission to raise the debt ceiling till the end of the year. I hope by then the few congressmen and senators that are configuring this legislation get the job done. All the negotiations are being done by several legislators, so what do we need the rest of them for? The government can save lots of money by getting rid of them. This sounds simplistic and silly and it is, but so are you and the rest of congress. You have obligations and time lines to follow, so let's get the job done. I will be glad to come to Washington and put these silly people in their place and mediate their silly arguments.

The ACA is a program without a measure of cost and you boxed yourself into doing it. There is no doubt that the health care system needs change and regulation, but passing the bill on Christmas Eve without due diligence has created front page headlines for a long time. The system has problems and if you are counting on the congress to help solve these problems, good luck.

The experts claim the federal exchange is working at 70% capacity. The fix is a long way off and this could send the ACA to Never Never Land. There were numerous warnings of the problems with the system and you chose to ignore them. These are not bumps in the road, they are sink holes. Between the shut down and the roll out of the ACA, you have created emotional and financial calamity in millions of American families' lives. This will not get you reelected, oh that's right, you can't be elected again. Master stroke of timing.

The bottom line is you should have had congress do their job long before the legislation was due. Now you instruct them to get the job done after they have caused this stress and made America look silly throughout the world. The exchange system that cost over 400 hundred million dollars is sending the ACA to an early fiscal disaster. You blame the House and the Senate and the extremist and I wonder how much of this could have been prevented if

October 13, 2013

President Barack Obama

1600 Pennsylvania Avenue N.W.

Washington D.C. 20500

Dear President Obama,

If you want to cut the spending cuts that are in place then you should be ready to repeal the ACA. The laws passed by you and congress should be followed, not altered at your every whim. You passed the laws that made the debt, now pay the bills and extend the debt ceiling as you need too. You are putting the country and the world in jeopardy by your foolish games. Do American people have the right to pick and choose their debt obligations after they signed contracts? I don't think so. You made the bills now pay the bills.

The deal that Kerry made with Afghanistan is not in the best interest of this country. Bring the troops home and let the Afgans solve their own problem. Stop borrowing money to solve other countries problems. Our taxes are for this country and the problems we have here. When America is on a solid foundation again, then selectively we can help other countries.

The ACA is turning into a train wreck because you, the congress and your administration did a lousy job putting together an important piece of legislation. The web site is a hacker's heaven and a customer's nightmare. The plan, designed to reduce cost, is increasing cost within the states, county by county and across the country. Counting on the young and healthy to run to the web site, that doesn't work, to register for health care is a major miscalculation. Why would a young person, many who can't find a job, want to add a monthly payment when they can pay a $95.00 tax and not have to register?

It is time for you to be responsible and instruct congress not to pass any laws they can't finance with existing revenues. The World Bank and the IMF have expressed grave concern for the silly games we are playing in Washington. Obviously your instructions to congress are not being followed. Simple, a clean CR and Debt Ceiling bill without restrictions. Resolve other matters with the guidelines, no money no legislation. Spend within our means.

October 14, 2013

President Barack Obama

1600 Pennsylvania Avenue N.W.

Washington D.C. 20500

Dear President Obama,

Researching and writing these letters every day has provided me with a clear picture of the media bias, the poor operation of the government and your inability to effectively perform the duties of the President of the United States. Media bias and poor government operations come and go with the immediate crisis. Your leadership style and managerial skills embarrass the country and create friction and controversy among Americans. You have managed to piss off every major religious, military and hard working group in America and you are a happy man. You are the leader of the me first generation and have demonstrated that throughout your presidency. Your crusade against the rich, while you are becoming rich, your blatant disregard for Christianity and the poor in this country, and your insistence on pushing a flawed ACA health care law, magnifies your agenda to ruin this country and the entrepreneurial spirit that made it great. You need to either step up to the challenges or step down.

The senate has come up with a potential solution to the debt crisis. Delaying the reinsurance tax and fixing the income verification of the ACA is placating to the democratic unions and throwing a bone to the republicans on the income verification which should have been resolved long ago. Simple, congress made the debt and they should pay the debt. The arguments should have taken place before they passed the spending bills and made them law. The best hope for the country is, bring home the troops and save that money, initiate tax reform to help create jobs, continue the current sequester law, work on a plan to fix or reform the ACA, perform their functions on a timely basis and don't spend it if you don't have it. Hopefully they will have enough sense to elect new leadership in the House and the Senate.

Sensible and independent women need to demand a stronger position in leadership in the House and Senate. Their loyalty should be to the country and not the party or specialist interest. Their organizational and fiscal management skills drive them to make better overall decisions in government matters. They sense the mood of the country and the people long before their counterparts and react quicker. The country need to give them the support they need and have earned. If you oppose this view, just take a hard look at the accomplishments of the male dominated congress.

October 15, 2013

President Barack Obama
1600 Pennsylvania Avenue N.W.
Washington D.C. 20500

Dear President Obama,

You and the congressional leaders are a bunch of inept clowns. You are an embarrassment to America and all the hard working people in this country. You are destroying our image as a powerful world leader. Children around the world are taught that you shouldn't spend more than you have and for some reason you bozoes can't understand this. Children around the world are taught to be responsible citizen and follow the laws and for some reason you and congress think you can pick and choose which laws you will follow. You put your political careers above the needs of the people and the country. Shameful, despicable group.

We have fiscal obligations to pay our bills. Pass a clean CR and Debt bill and get the process done. Do not pass any other legislation until you resolve the fiscal matters and resolve to only spend the revenue you collect. Take on the entitlement programs and make necessary adjustments over the long term to resolve the problems they will encounter. Repeal the ACA and take the loss on a bill that is filled with problems, misinterpretation, waivers and exemptions. The ACA is a disaster that started before its implementation. Seek professional help from qualified professionals that can show congress how to do a realistic budget.

Mr. President, to help get out of this fiscal mess you have to bring in professionals who know how to create Jobs. The numbers your administration produce are a crock of crap. The fact that the stock market is up is because the companies trimmed their budgets by letting American workers go and increased their profits. Jobs and manufacturing need to come back to America. The more jobs, the more tax revenue, the quicker the deficit will reduce and you will have the ability to expand the budget, not go over it.

Another part of the fiscal problem that must be resolved is tax reform, waste, fraud and mismanagement in government. It would make sense to spend money to find the waste and fraud and bring it under control. If you spend a billion dollars to collect 10 billion dollars and stop the fraud that created this problem, it makes sense. Stop blaming others and start leading.

October 16, 2013

President Barack Obama
1600 Pennsylvania Avenue N.W.
Washington D.C. 20500

Dear President Obama,

Praising politicians for work they should have accomplished two months ago on legislation that goes nowhere and moves the clock ahead, exemplifies your lack of leadership and the work of your administration. Americans suffered while political games were being played. The last time I looked the congress and you were paid by the American taxpayers. It aggravates me to hear these state representatives and senators talk about their constituents and why they are in Washington. They are paid by every American and are supposed to represent every American. The oath they took is to uphold the Constitution, not the state they represent. That goes for you also. You need to stop worrying about the Democratic Party and do the job you were elected to do and that is, the President of the United States of America. Your personal agenda has no place in your duties as President.

It is time for every American to step up and get involved for the country. We will all have to give back until the fiscal crisis is solved in this country. It will be easier to give back small amounts now, rather than risk loosing entire programs down the road. Americans need to push for efficient government, zero waste, prosecuted fraud, and legitimate tax reform. The ACA with all its good intent is a perfect example. The cost of the health care web site was set to cost 93.7 million dollars. It is up to 292 million dollars and doesn't work. The President should say stop until the problems are fixed and this open ended contract is reviewed and corrected. This is a gross misappropriation of money.

Mr. President, what part of math did you miss in school? It will be necessary for you to make difficult decisions, even if it affects your beloved Obamacare. The conference committee will need your full support to accomplish change. This hostage crap you pulled on the House isn't going to work when they come up with a lagitament plan to put America's finances in order. Prepare yourself to make concessions and compromises or have your own plan ready to present to the committee before the deadline. Don't get on the extreme bandwagon when you know we are dealing with an extreme problem. It is time to stop borrowing money and produce a budget on a timely basis that is equal to revenue.

October 17, 2013

President Barack Obama

1600 Pennsylvania Avenue N.W.

Washington D.C. 20500

Dear President Obama,

    The, to do list, of immigration, the food bill and the budget has only one priority and that is the budget and getting the fiscal policy of the country in order. How can you plan any other legislation until you know how much you have to spend? Once the budget is established, then the appropriate cuts will have to be made to stay in line with the budget. Your administration has wasted more money on energy, health care and the misguided SNAP Program than any other administration that I can remember. The priority is to get the fiscal problem solved and you should be working with the committee to do this. Don't come up with the," I won't be held hostage by the conference committee," excuse when you don't like what they present.

    The people, poor and rich, will have to make sacrifices to help pay down the debt and control spending. They are tired of watching the politicians using spending as a tool to get reelected. Start by eliminating matching funds for political candidates at every level of government. Part of the budget process should include tax reform and employee benefit reform for programs that the government can't continue to afford. Estimated waste, fraud and poor management should be cut from the agencies budgets in an effort to get control over their spending. If they don't have it, like most families in America, maybe they will make better choices in how to spend it.

    The ACA must be stopped and fixed. Your stubbornness and lack of transparency is going to send this program down in flames. I and I am sure there are others, are tired of watching money being wasted on a program that has the potential to be great but has the direction and management that will cost America and American dearly. You need to do the right thing and make a deal with the congress for a guaranteed fix and reinstatement of the program. There needs to be a common sense approach to fixing and managing this program and everyone has to be on board, including the insurance companies and the medical industry. Mismanagement and money will not cure the Affordable Care Act and you know that.

October 18, 2013

President Barack Obama

1600 Pennsylvania Avenue N.W.

Washington D.C. 20500

Dear President Obama,

Spin this any way you want, but the facts are the facts and the Health Care web site is a monster out of control. Sebelius and Chao can avoid testifying for only so long and then it will be judgment day. The system that is costing a half a billion dollars is a runaway train looking for a wall to crash into and from the reports of the failure to fix it, anytime soon would be my best guess.

Forget the web site, what are you going to do about the increased co pays, very high deductibles, out of network doctor fees, the poor that will not be covered by Medicaid, and most of all the lack of participation by the younger generation. That tech generation is not going to waste time on a confused and flawed web site. Worst of all you have the hard right digging in and going for the kill of a dysfunctional program. Stop, fix, and cut a deal before it is too late. You can't hide Sebelius, Chao and the facts forever.

The new debt cap will be about 17.3 trillion dollars. What are you going to do when other countries stop buying the debt or you run out of paper to print money on? What are you going to do if other countries decide that the American dollar needs to be replaced as the world economic measure? Should you be sitting down with the conference committee on budget and debt ceiling solutions or are you going to let some of your inept administration people do that? Will you continue the no hostage approach? The next shutdown is on you because you agreed to the conference, but we know that doesn't mean much if you don't like what they have to offer.

The Whitehouse tours will begin again on a limited basis in November, that's a good thing, the people's house is open for tours but not for business. Does this mean you will consider reopening the transparency you promised?

October 19, 2013

President Barack Obama

1600 Pennsylvania Avenue N.W.

Washington D.C. 20500

Dear President Obama,

Calling for bipartisan cooperation after what you did to the country and shut down the government is the height of hypocrisy. Don't try to hide behind your effort to help the uninsured when you left millions of the poorest people without any avenue to get insurance, even Medicaid. The early results you are hiding indicates the train has left the track, billions have been wasted, and millions will be without insurance again. In case you and your advisors missed it, the insurance companies have stuck it to you with higher premiums and huge deductibles.

You want cooperation, time for a deal. The world is angry over our 17 trillion dollars deficit and the last set of political games. Countries all over the world are suffering economic problems and cutting back and here we sit wanting to dry up the monetary funds by borrowing more money. Our fiscal policies have created the hate these countries have for us. So here is the deal, the debt ceiling has to be raised to meet our obligations, and we need to establish a budget that will reverse the negative trend and put us on a positive track to debt reduction and sound fiscal policy. If this requires you to stop and fix the ACA and have another shutdown, so be it until the country is put on a sound financial foundation.

The so called ass kicking you gave congress only put the fight off for three months. It is the same congress and they are more determined than ever to solve the fiscal problems they have created over the years. They won't have to worry about the ACA because that is in a nose dive and will crash on its own. You should have read the bill before you signed it. That seems to be a bad habit you have, especially when it comes to the veterans. You held the American people hostage over a failing ACA and that is all you have to give up. Do yourself a favor, if this does happen again, don't put up fences around open air national monuments. That was dumb and whoever advised you to do that is dumber.

October 20, 2013

President Barack Obama

1600 Pennsylvania Avenue N.W.

Washington D.C. 20500

Dear President Obama,

Your proposal to use the Consumer Price Index to limit Social Security payments makes sense, but what really needs to be done is all the entitlement programs need to be reduced by one percent. This should be structured with lower gas and food prices to make up the difference. The democrats that signed a letter taking a hard line against the CPI limits are part of the reason we are 17 trillion dollars in debt. The budget process will have to be an assortment of entitlement cuts, tax reform, job creation, viable waste and fraud programs, and bringing home the troops. This country can't afford other country's wars without remuneration. The release of 1.6 billion dollars in aid to Pakistan is a slap in the face to all Americans who suffered during the shutdown.

You should make your position very clear at the beginning of the budget committee so they don't waste any time chasing reforms that are not acceptable. The country should not have to face another shutdown because of ideological differences. The extremist on the right and left have to move to the center and support the budget committee's reforms and budget. Everything should be on the table including the ACA.

Over 400 million dollars was spent setting up the web site for the ACA. There are numerous problems with the site that will take weeks to repair according to the experts. I hope it isn't the same experts that designed the site. What gem in your administration signed an open ended contract that raised the cost for the web site from 93.7 million dollars to over 400 million dollars? There is an old saying that crap in is crap out and this is what we have, a pile of crap. You can stand on the Whitehouse lawn all day with the few people that have insurance from the ACA, but I want to see you stand on the lawn with all the people you left out and can't get insurance thru the ACA. Who is getting fired over this 400 million dollar pile of junk?

Sometimes you have to admit you are wrong and start over again. It works a lot better than going down with the ship and then people won't have to say, "Barack Who."

October 21, 2013

President Barack Obama

1600 Pennsylvania Avenue N.W.

Washington D.C. 20500

Dear President Obama,

Sebelius is going to testify, how nice. What could go wrong has gone wrong for the ACA. I wonder if someone is trying to tell us something. You promised transparency, what is this going to cost the American taxpayer and how long is it going to take? I hope Sebelius will have an answer or will she say, it doesn't matter, we need to fix the problem. I wonder, what does matter in Washington?

The Saudi's are angry over our handling of the Syrian and Iranian problems. I know the Middle East countries own 173 billion dollars of our debt, but why don't they fix their own problems over there? They need us to protect them from aggression by their neighboring countries, so maybe they need to shut up or put up with their blood and money. Oil is not holding us hostage any longer.

Pull all our military forces out of the Middle East and be ready to help Israel if necessary. Stop supplying weapons and money to our enemies. What have we achieved in those countries other than to give a back door to the extremist and create civil war? The drone strikes are causing civilian casualties and that is what a bomb usually does. The people know who the bad guys are, so stay away, because eventually the drone will fly and hit its intended target.

I am working on a budget that will put America on a positive fiscal trend. I believe it will be something you agree with and will save your ACA from a drone attack. It matters who will have to suffer minor financial setbacks so I will offset them with reduced personal expenditures. I hope to have this done before the December 13, deadline for your review and approval. It will eliminate us having to borrow any more money and pay down the debt. However, I don't know of anything that will stop Washington from spending the surpluses other than replacing all of congress with common sense housewives.

October 22, 2013

President Barack Obama

1600 Pennsylvania Avenue N.W.

Washington D.C. 20500

Dear President Obama,

You appealed to the Organization of America to continue their support of Obamacare and you brought in Jeffery Zients to help fix the website. You have managed to spend millions of dollars on a defunct system, millions of dollars on advertising and navigators, have left over five million of the poorest people without an avenue to get insurance, the insurance companies had to cancel hundreds of thousands insurance policies because they don't meet minimum standards, the copays are high and the deductibles are in the thousands and there is a glitch in the law that only state exchange enrollees will get subsidies and that is being challenged in the court.

The Supreme Court gave you a gift when you changed the fine into a tax. They slapped you when they allowed the states to choose Medicaid expansion and thus leaving five million plus poor people without insurance. Now you will argue the law intended that everyone was eligible for a subsidy. If the Supreme Court interprets the law on strict language, you lose, and you will need congress to change the wording in the law, good luck with that one. Make a deal, stop it, and fix it and do it right or continue your trip in the Titanic.

Like the ACA, the situation in Syria is a mess. The rebels are losing and they don't want to come to the table to talk, bold bunch. Is this because there are too many rebel groups. The Saudi's are angry, so let them deal with the problem. Again, stop supplying weapons in a religious war, we will be the big losers in this.

You should tell the High Courts in the Dominican Republic, if they don't considering changing their position on children born in the Dominican, you will cut off all aid to the country. Children born there to illegal immigrants are considered illegal also. This sounds like the court wants to set up a specific class of people as citizens. There is a prominent right side to this issue and I hope you follow it.

October 23, 2013

President Barack Obama

1600 Pennsylvania Avenue N.W.

Washington D.C. 20500

Dear President Obama,

    Your advisors are meeting with the insurance company CEO's, a little late don't you think. I know there must have been prior meetings, but it doesn't seem like you accomplished much. In your collegian studies, did you miss the part about how free enterprise is stronger and better prepared to handle customer's needs and wants? Beside the failure of the website, you limited the competition in the states and you drove up the prices on the people living in the rural areas. The competition should have gone national, across state lines and premiums would reflect the competition. It's not too late.

    The genius in your administration that decided people should open accounts and expose their information to an unsecure site before they browsed the site for insurance product, is either stupid or dumb like a fox. Even if they don't enroll you have all their information that you can share with other agencies. Spying Again? Is Sebelius the goat that is covering up for one or more of your advisors?

    What nerve you have asking the congress to move on immigration reform. The budget and the debt ceiling are the first priority and your administration has demonstrated they can't do more than one thing at a time and get it right. I won't ask you to delay Obamacare anymore because I'm convinced you aren't smart enough to do that or you want to lose more seats in the house at election time. Focus on the budget and do something positive about Obamascare, because both pieces of legislation are scaring, confusing, and frustrating the American people.

    I wonder why we spend an average of $7500.00 per person on healthcare, Japan spends $2729.00, Canada spends $4079.00 and the UK spends $3129.00 on healthcare. Japan, Canada, and the UK cover all their citizens and regulate the costs. Their care may not be as good as ours, but they seem to live longer, maybe it has something to do with personal responsibility. What do you think, Mr. President?

October 24, 2013

President Barack Obama

1600 Pennsylvania Avenue N.W.

Washington D.C. 20500

Dear President Obama,

The website builders turned on your administration before the dime hit the ground. The people responsible for picking CGI and QSSI should be fired. They started with a 94 million dollar contract that ended up costing over 400 million dollars and the damn thing doesn't work. The advisors that gave the green light to the application process should go along with them. You can tell your fellow democrat, Frank Palone of New Jersey, that the only monkey at the hearing was him. I guess his advisors forgot to tell him that thousands of people in New Jersey lost their insurance because of the ACA requirements. A pinnacle display of political intelligence.

Your proposed compromise on immigration reform and willingness to consider the house version is a step in the right direction, but I wouldn't encourage the congress to do anything until the budget and debt legislation is done. I would like to see how compromising you are on that first. The congress should load the immigration bill with triggers to make sure the process is followed and the people support it. You must control the border, get the immigrants to register, and have them sponsor a voluntary language requirement, then follow the normal path to citizenship. They must be willing to do their part and prove they will not be a burden on society.

Your proposal to delay the sanctions on Iran are a mistake. Show me some demonstrative intent while we talk and lift the new sanctions in stages that coincide with their dismantling of their nuclear program. If the Iranian's can't agree to that then the sanctions should pass and be enforced. Talk has always been cheap in the Middle East and I don't see that changing.

Accelerate the program to bring the troops home, it is the right thing to do and you will need the money you save to help prevent the ACA from a monetary death. Eventually, fixing the website isn't the answer to the success of the program, it needs to be fixed and I don't see much cooperation coming your way on that unless you demonstrate real compromise in the budget, debt and later the immigration legislation. Good Luck.

October 25, 2013

President Barack Obama

1600 Pennsylvania Avenue N.W.

Washington D.C. 20500

You are absolutely right, the country has two different visions. Keeping America number one in the world and providing opportunity for every hard working American is first and foremost. Then there is your version, Me first and what is good for the democrats next. Your pompous attitude and payback to the Democratic Party who put you in office signals one direction, social engineering and dependency on the federal government. Yes there are two visions for this country and unfortunately you and the democrats have two votes and the republican's one vote and America no votes. Most of you are a disgraceful bunch who put yourself before your country.

You must have stopped in Washington State and loaded up on free weed if you think the website is the only problem with Obamacare. Millions are left without insurance, millions are having their policy canceled and the high premiums and deductibles are like having no insurance at all. If you can't afford the premiums, how can you afford a $10,000.00 deductible? How can you afford a $45.00 co pay? No the website is not the only problem with Obamacare and if you think the other visionaries are going to support changes in the law for you, take another puff and dream about it. You created the division, now live with it.

What a revelation, we spy on other countries. We spy on ourselves and our political enemies here and abroad and so does the rest of the world. The difference is we got caught. In the real scheme of things, other countries like the information they get from us as much as we like getting it. There are bad guys everywhere and if you are doing something that you don't want anyone to know about, maybe you shouldn't be doing it. Spying is the necessary ugly side of government and it has been going on since the beginning of time, get over it.

October 26, 2013

Dear President Obama,

The Saudi's are worried about you turning your back on them while you negotiate with Iran, to the Saudi's I say, welcome to the land of broken promises. What makes them think you have their best interest at heart when you don't even have that for America? I know you have a tough job, but your decision process is flawed and the information and advice from your advisors has one direction, me first. After writing you 300 hundred letters, nothing you do surprises me. The media loves you because you keep the rating up.

Sebelius sees a silver lining in the health care website. What is so great about the people's information being unsecure and tied to the social security and IRS hub? This is a hacker's dream come true and they see gold in them there hills. Sebelius can spin it anyway she wants, it still measures up to a 400 hundred million dollar debacle and counting. It is amazing that we need more time to fix a system they built over three years and it is supposed to be fixed in 30 days. Government efficiency.

Governor Como raised the standards of the teachers in New York, maybe you should get a copy of that method and use it in your administration then distribute it to congress. The politicians need it as much or more than the teachers. Every child getting a good education will help solve the problems in the poor class of people. Another solution would be to tell Hollywood and the game designers to curb the violence in their media and encourage kids to smell the fresh air. I must say you are a good example to follow for that. Maybe we need to see you play golf and basketball more often.

October 27, 2013

President Barack Obama

1600 Pennsylvania Avenue N.W.

Washington D.C. 20500

Dear President Obama,

Do you think someone up there is trying to tell you something, now the hub, run by Verizon that connects all the states with the main information center crashed? I would take that as a sign of divine direction. I would give it some consideration.

Susan Rice has come up with a plan for a better foreign policy. I didn't know you had a foreign policy. It seems you operate on a crisis by crisis basis, just like you do at home with the congress. Here is the best foreign policy, bring the troops home and let the people solve their own problems. The internet is doing a better job of promoting democracy and sparking change.

The conference committee will finally meet on the budget and debt limit legislation. You are not in a good position if they can't agree on a deal as the second set of sequestration cuts will kick in. Do you think the first shut down was worth protecting Obamacare or was that more important than creating jobs, keeping a strong military and putting the country on a sound and responsible financial road. Time will tell and the elections will be the judge.

The food stamp program, SNAP, needs a major overhaul. The abuse and fraud in the program is rampant and the changes the congress is suggesting, means testing, able body men who can work plus a structured program that allows for specific food purchases, will reduce the cost of the program and continue the benefits for the people that really need them. It will also be a bargaining chip for you in the budget battle.

The FDA tightened the grip on prescription drugs. This only took about six years, but better late than never. It might also reduce the cost of Medicare and Medicaid as a side benefit. It will definitely increase the population in the legal marijuana states, unless you decide to enforce the law of the land or the law of your choice, can't figure that one out.

October 28, 2013

Dear President Obama,

The art of spying is not to get caught. I am sure all the previous presidents did the same thing you are doing, but they didn't get caught. When you lie to the American people, you can keep your insurance and many other misrepresentations, and you know you will get caught, do it at the end of your term in office so the problem falls on the next president. Some people will lose their insurance, thousands of people will lose their insurance and they can't be reinstated. This is a paperwork nightmare. The opp's factor is only going to work so long and then it catches up to you and it looks like you are a hub in a wheel and everything is headed your way.

Who elected Citigroup to write legislation changing the Dodd Frank bill? The retiree bill that calls for reduced standards and the derivative legislation need to be vetoed. The clowns on Wall Street want to gamble, send them to Las Vegas with their own money. It is time to stop Wall Street from investing on failures, or insurance as they call it. We don't need another 2008.

Lindsey Graham is going to block nominations until you come clean on Benghazi. This is not something you can let go till the end of your term. It is time to man up, if you can live with Obamacare on the front pages, maybe Benghazi will go to page four. The entire incident smells of cover up and I know it will affect the 2016 presidential election, or are you keeping quiet because it doesn't matter. You wait long enough, you can dump it in Hillary's lap and she can take the blame.

The budget talks should produce solid fiscal agreements, not modest agreements. This has to be knock down, hard research, and commonsense conclusions, not a Lilly De Ponce showcase. Every department and agency should do their share. I continue to support the case for have the best five business schools come up with a solution and pass it on to congress. Let the kids who have to pay the bill down the road have a fair shot at balancing the budget and reducing the debt. Put the challenge out there, but it might take more than thirty days. No guts, no glory.

October 29, 2013

President Barack Obama

1600 Pennsylvania Avenue N.W.

Washington D.C. 20500

Dear President Obama,

When the New York Times runs an article about who is in charge, you have something to worry about. The rumor mill is running and the stories are fascinating. Maybe you should consider less advice from Valarie and Michelle and more advice from the American people. Lord know you haven't listened to anything I have to say or you wouldn't be in this mess. A perplexing question, what does he know and is he in charge? That book will look good in your presidential library.

There is no point in brow beating you about Obamacare any longer. The plan and results speak for themselves, not to mention the waste of billions of dollars. It is beyond my comprehension how you can stand and tell the people to be patient. Do you really believe half the things you say?

Your fellow democrats always talk about the needy people and how they have to look out for their needs. What a crock of crap. They ignored them in Obamacare, they will lose benefits in the SNAP program because of the waste and fraud and pending cuts, and they have not benefited from the 77 billion dollars in the education budget. The democrats care about one thing, votes that will keep them in power to make people reliant on government.

A perfect example of the problems in your administration is watching and listening to the representatives you send to testify for congress. They never give a straight answer and they sound like kids that got caught with their hands in the cookie jar. They can't remember who they talk to or who authorized anything, but they promise everything will be better. It is embarrassing to the country to watch these people adjust the truth to cover up for other people's stupidity. I can't give a good reason to any other government wanting to become a democracy to follow our form of democracy. What is simpler than telling the truth?

October 30, 2013

President Barack Obama

1600 Pennsylvania Avenue N.W.

Washington D.C. 20500

Dear President Obama,

Iraq wants more military aid and technical support and if we don't give it to them they will ask the Russians or the Chinese. A bold statement before they even ask for help. Tell them to deal with their own problems and get help where ever they can. We shed enough blood and money over there, we don't need any more of their crap.

The bad apple insurance companies are the blame for people losing their insurance policies, which one of your spin jockeys came up with that crock of manure? Do you take the blame for anything, like maybe you should have read the bill before you signed it? Even if you had there is still the comprehension factor so you would have signed it anyway. Stop blaming everyone for your short comings. You wanted the job, you have it, so start doing it.

Is everybody happy? The budget talks started and everyone is happy. Nothing accomplished, but everyone is happy. Let's see, the young people have to worry about a 17 trillion dollar debt, they have to sign up for health insurance to help pay the bills for the old people, they will not see social security or Medicare because they are going broke, and they have to live home longer because they can't find jobs. How many young people do you have at the budget talks?

It is time to concentrate on waste, fraud, tax reform and the stupid regulations that allow people who are worth millions and pay no taxes. It is time for everyone to pay something and eliminate tax credits for sitting home. Tell the happy people that spending is out of hand and the young are ready to revolt. Maybe that will wake them up because the day is coming. You can't keep taking more from the smaller younger generations and expect them to be happy. Just hope you are out of office before they wake up.

October 31, 2013

President Barack Obama

1600 Pennsylvania Avenue N.W.

Washington D.C. 20500

Dear President Obama,

This is the first, after 300 hundred letters, I reviewed my sources and there was not a negative word about you from your ardent supporters. Passing out candy at the Whitehouse was the big headline. Of course, that doesn't mean all your issues have gone away, they are not selling newspapers right now.

Tax reform and jobs will go a long way to helping the country recover that is real tax reform and jobs not the spin the Whitehouse sells as jobs created. I know you have worked on tax reform, you proved that by the 51 new taxes in the health care law. Take a hard look at the 4,000 top earners that don't pay any taxes, the movie industry which enjoys mega tax breaks, the oil industry, and the financial industry which charges you for electronic trade both ways. Then there are the major companies like your friends at GE that pay a pittance to government after all the government contracts we give them. The rule for real tax reform should be that everyone must pay something, none of this 40 plus percent that don't pay anything.

The happy people that are working on the budget and debt legislation need to come up with a long term agreement that will help the country. I agree with you on this, but let's not lose our head over my support. I keep hearing how the rich are providing the jobs with their investments. I think there should be a heavy tax on day traders and investments that out of the country. I wonder how much of the billions of dollars that are traded everyday actually turn into real investment capital for companies in America. Lately, I talk to more foreign people on the phone about local problems, why is that?

Keep in mind, the younger generations can't pay the 17 trillion dollar debt, afford to go to college and pay that loan, afford to live on their own in a reflective lifestyle and buy your insurance to help the old people. There needs to be a smart balance for a healthy economy.

Francismdelvecchio.com

November 1, 2013

President Barack Obama

1600 Pennsylvania Avenue N.W.

Washington D.C. 20500

Dear President Obama,

Iraq wants military aid and technical support, did they bring their checkbook or will we continue to cut our military so we can supply those weapons? Did you ever wonder where Al Qaeda is getting their money? Why can't we stop the flow of money and weapons to them? None of them look like their starving and they seem to have an endless supply of weapons. Are we spying on the right people?

Your fellow democrats are worried about their reelection in 2014 because of Obamacare. They are not worried about the people who can't get insurance or the people losing their insurance, just worried about their reelection. What a feckless bunch they are. The GOP is just as bad, they are going to watch this shooting star fall from the sky. They are wallowing in your misery and loving it and the people are suffering anxiety attacks wondering if they will have insurance. You can fix the website all you want but you will never be able to fix the damage you are doing to the Democratic Party, good job.

Here is some good news, Rand Paul and Ted Cruz are sniping at each other. Soon Christie will jump in and the GOP will shoot themselves in the foot like they always do and limp into the 2016 election. However, I expect that the GOP will capitalize on, it doesn't matter, whatever, and you can keep your insurance and your doctor, as usual, it will turn into a three ring circus.

You claim the deficit is falling, what part of a balanced budget don't you understand? The deficit will fall when we have a balanced budget and the 17 trillion we owe starts to get repaid. I won't hold my breath waiting for this to happen. I repeat my claim, the young generation will wake up and you will see a march on Washington that will make Woodstock look like a get together.

Francismdelvecchio.com

November 2, 2013

President Barack Obama

1600 Pennsylvania Avenue N.W.

Washington D.C. 20500

Dear President Obama,

Egypt and Iraq are looking for new partners for arms and aid. I would probably look there also, knowing that the Russian debt is 2.5% of GDP and America is at 100% of GDP and we owe them about 138 billion dollars. Considering we can't do a budget on time or control our spending, it would only make sense for Egypt and Iraq to look elsewhere. I don't think they will be bringing their checkbook to Russia either.

Schumer has endorsed Hillary Clinton for president, well how do you do, one die hard supporting another die hard democrat. What does it matter, it doesn't, so why do it now? She needs the donors and the dollars. She ran up a campaign debt in 2008 and struck a deal with you so you could run. Did you pay off her campaign debts with your donations? Before you jump on her band wagon make sure Obamacare is operating smoothly or she will feed you to the fishes. There is nothing sacred in politics.

One in five Afgans are drug addicts now. I am surprised the number isn't higher as they are a major producer of illegal drugs. I wonder what the Muslin religion states about drug addicts or terrorists that use their people as human bombs. Maybe you can ask them the next time you have them to the Whitehouse for breakfast. Has the Pope been invited for breakfast? Come to think of it, I haven't seen too many Rabbis or Ministers either.

We are improving our relations with the Chinese, this is a good think since we owe them over a trillion dollars. Are we paying them off in gold or is that a big secret? I think it is time for a gold inventory at Fort Knox. They are still upset with us about our human rights position and telling them they should do more for their people. I don't know if I would listen to us about human rights since we have over a million abortions every year. It's not like we don't have poor, homeless, starving people living here. Makes you wonder.

Francismdelvecchio.com

November 3, 2013

President Barack Obama

1600 Pennsylvania Avenue N.W.

Washington D.C. 20500

Dear President Obama,

I can't believe you trucked over to Virginia to campaign for the democratic nominee whose name is not worth mentioning. You jumped all over the Tea Party for the government shut down, but don't you think your time would be better served if you were talking to the people on the budget conference or talking to some corporate leaders who can help create jobs. When are you going to get off the blame trail?

Millions can be covered for free under Obamacare, but the poorest in some states are left without any coverage. If a person wants to pay a $40.00 t0 $60.00 dollar copay and a $6300.00 deductible, go for it, but they should not be allowed to claim medical bankruptcy if they can't meet the minimums. Most seniors have $100.00 deducted from their social security for Medicare, why should anyone get insurance for nothing, especially when most of the money to pay for it will come from the Medicare budget. Able body people who can work should pay a portion of their medical expense, so should people that get food stamps for nothing because they are too lazy to work.

Thousands of Iranians protested in front of the old embassy in Iran. They hate America and will interrupt any talks we have with the unpopular government there. We do not need any more controversy than we have now. Try supporting our friends in the region if we have any left.

The voter registration law is coming up in Wisconsin for trial, if people can go to concerts, movies, parties, show up for protest and other civil matters, then why can't they get their butt over to get the right documentation and register to vote?

The best President of the United States is a person who gets things done for the benefit of the people and the country and you never know they are there. That is not you.

Francismdelvecchio.com

November 4, 2013

President Barack Obama

1600 Pennsylvania Avenue N.W.

Washington D.C. 20500

Dear President Obama,

The federal law suit regarding voter rights is giving people an easy path to shun their personal   responsibility. Wanting to do something and having to do something are the issues here. The IRS says you have to maintain your records for seven years, you need a birth certificate to get married or get a driver's license, you need a birth certificate to get a passport and you are responsible for maintaining these records. You will require similar records for voter registration, the difference being what you have to do versus what you want to do. Why should the requirements be waived because you don't want to produce the same records? The problems you face now must have come up before in your personal matters.

Why are we constantly making laws that require us to pay taxes so we can get them back at a later date in tax credits and refunds? That seems counterproductive to me. This also opens the possibility of cheating on your tax return and who doesn't take advantage of that. The tax code needs major reform and this would make doing a budget more realistic. The simple process of keeping the money you have and not paying more money or waiting for a refund makes sense to me.

Legislation is going forward so people can keep their insurance and their doctors until the end of 2014. Delos Cosgrove, CEO of the renowned Cleveland Clinic, stated that the 2700 hundred page ACA has another 27,000 pages of regulations and is forcing doctors and hospitals to make changes. The marginal hospitals will go under putting more pressure on the other medical facilities. This legislation should go past 2014 and be made permanent, but that would send Obamacare to an early demise. Good luck with this passing.

The legislation to stop employer discrimination against gay people has passed step one in the Senate and sent to the House. Successful executives hire successful people, because money follows money, not prejudices.

Francismdelvecchio.com

November 5, 2013

President Barack Obama

1600 Pennsylvania Avenue N.W.

Washington D.C. 20500

Dear President Obama,

Credibility, a nation listens to its leader lie and still wants to follow him down a path of destruction. It is amazing how many people are willing to bet on a health care bill that started with 2,700 pages in the congress and has another 27,000 pages of regulations and you can't keep the insurance you like. The grass is not greener on the other side of the hill, it was just loaded with more crap to make you think it is greener. The government can't give you something unless it takes it from someone else. Hold on seniors, it is your turn to payback and there is nothing you can do about it.

Every time a crisis evolves there was always some kind of warning that people didn't heed. The President knew people were going to lose their insurance and he lied about it to your face and is laughing behind your back. You can get new insurance along with the 51 new taxes it brings with Obamacare. The joke is on us and we continue to elect crooked politicians like Mc Auliffe in Virginia and listen to a President that has lied his way into the Hall of Shame. Who is really pushing his buttons or is he that dumb.

Mr. President, you slam the Tea Party for their extremism, but what people can't see is they are the warning. Black Americans complain about stop and frisk in New York and here you are picking the pockets of every American and they can't see it. The fallacy in your plan is you could never take enough from the people that have it and give it to the people that don't, because the harsh reality is people like you need the rich to put you in office so you can manage the masses through government regulation.

Someday the money will run out and you won't have to worry about shutting down the government, it will self-destruct like all other great empires. I hope you are around to get your just rewards.

November 6, 2013

President Barack Obama

1600 Pennsylvania Avenue N.W.

Washington D.C. 20500

Dear President Obama,

The Senate can pass all the laws they want about discrimination against gays in the work place, when you have a personal issue coupled with a religious issue, it isn't going to change how people feel. It all boils down to the interview and the employer's preference. This law will create grievous aggravation between the employers and gays that have great working relationships. Good executives hire people for their talent, not their sexual orientation. Another waste of time when the budget and debt deadline are the priority.

The senate democrats can have all the private meetings they want with you about Obamacare and their reelection, it is not about them, it's about what you want. They are jumping ship and right now they are probably hoping you go down with the ship. The people are worried, the insurance companies are worried, and the politicians are scared, so stop trying to sell the Edsel, it isn't going to happen.

Billionaires getting farm subsidies, 11.3 million dollars over the past 17 years. I think it is time to look at reform and justified spending cuts before they past the long overdue Agriculture Bill, makes common sense.

Iran will stop its nuclear program if the U.S. gives them relief from economic sanctions. We can put that next to you stopping Obamacare and that isn't going to happen. Their buying time and resupplying. Down the road you will hear they still hate us and their religious leader wants to start the nuclear program again. They have never seemed to be a nation that wastes money like our government does, maybe they are short on the lender supply.

The republicans want to help you out a bit, the want to bring in a more moderate opponent, similar to dumbing down. They won in Virginia, but too dumb to figure it out.

Francismdelvecchio.com

November 7, 2013

President Barack Obama

1600 Pennsylvania Avenue N.W.

Washington D.C. 20500

Dear President Obama,

Apologies are not going to help people that need medical coverage. They are not going to help people that can't afford the new coverage. You and your administration officials are the most despicable, heartless bunch of hooligans ever to step a foot into the Whitehouse. You can fix the technical problems with the website, but how are you going to fix the emotional and fiscal stress you have put at every American's doorstep. This is going to turn into a fiscal nightmare for the country and a complicated and legal mess for the medical industry. Lenin stated that socialized medicine is the Keystone to the arch of a socialist state and that is what it looks like here.

There were reports how the IRS sent out over 4 billion dollars in fraudulent tax returns. A Lithuanian address received 655 refunds at one address and 433 at another. An address in Shanghai received 343 refunds. Two Orlando addresses received 580 and 291 refunds. Other cities like Detroit, Chicago, Atlanta and Houston had similar results. The IRS claimed they were too quick to send out refunds. This is all due to identity theft. Over 1.6 million cases of fraud have been identified this year and the problem is getting worse.

The report stated they are trying to fix the problem and having better success, but it takes about 120 days before they can verify the right person for the refund. Two points, one if there were no tax refunds there would not be a problem. It never made any sense to send money to the government and wait for a refund. This dictates that tax reform should be a priority. Point two, if the IRS takes over 120 days to verify a person for a refund, why on earth did you select them to run Obamacare and be a part of income verification which isn't getting done. There needs to be serious tax reform and government accountability.

Mr. President, the best indicator of how well something is managed, is how well it operates when you are not there. However, in your case I don't think it matters whether you and your administration are on the job or not, your focus is on changing government not operating it efficiently. You were not elected to change our way of life, but to make it better, disappointing.

Francismdelvecchio.com

November 8, 2013

President Barack Obama

1600 Pennsylvania Avenue N.W.

Washington D.C. 20500

Dear President Obama,

You are sticking it to the poor again. The DSH, disproportionate share hospital program, will be cut by 500 million dollars in 2014. This was all dependent on the enrollments goals for the Obamacare. The enrollment isn't going to happen, the cuts are going through, the hospitals that serve the poor will suffer under the strain and cut services, and the consumer will have to pick up the tab through higher premiums. This program will cut over 5.5 billion dollars over the next 5 years. Great foresight.

You have two major pieces of legislation to worry about, the budget and debt bill and the Affordable Care Act, which is really the unaffordable care act. This is not the time to worry about Cuban Policy. This will not take Obamacare off the front page because it has too many problems. I told you to delay and fix it and you didn't listen.

You have your staff working on a solution for people to keep their health care. I suggest you bring in some professionals to do that because the track record of your staff's performance is like the junk falling from space, the impact is catastrophic.

The immigration bill isn't going to be done this year because there are only 16 day left to the congressional session. The bill is a victim of priorities, health is more important than legal rights and nothing works without money, besides, you will need something to blow your horn about in 2014, the election year. Wake up immigrants, the republicans are not the problem, you are the meat on next year's plate.

There is a common sense solution to the problems that plaque the country, I am in complete agreement with the Rickmister, Tax reform, a flat tax with everyone paying something and term limits on congress without lifetime benefits. Common sense, what's that?

Francismdelvecchio.com

November 9, 2013

President Barack Obama

1600 Pennsylvania Avenue N.W.

Washington D.C. 20500

Dear President Obama,

Health Sherpa, built a website so people could browse the different insurance products in three days. The problem that Ning Liang doesn't understand, is that is not the intent of the national health care site. It is about gathering information and conjuring up votes for the Democratic Party. What store have you gone into recently asked to see your money or credit card before you shopped or any other American? What is transparent about this administration is what you are trying to do to this country and the people. What is more revolting is how those democrats, you had a private meeting with, were more concerned about their butts than they were about the people that are losing their insurance. What a ship of fools we have elected.

Susan Rice suggested America pay its back dues and become a voting member in UNESCO again, the education, science, and culture arm of the United Nations. This is another waste of money. The U.S. does enough to help the world and as soon as the money stops the friendship stops. Egypt is a perfect example. We need to do a better job of supporting our children's education here first.

Iran's leader, Rouhani, won't give up the uranium enrichment program in the nuclear talks in Geneva which have produced nothing but hot air. This is the same delaying tactic the North Koreans used to push their nuclear program ahead. Going back to the talks in ten days, don't waste the jet fuel. They have no intention of altering their master program, they just want the sanctions lifted.

What is the point of offering the Palestinians another 75 million dollars to continue the peace talks? The Israelis acquired the land in question during the war and now they are going to build settlements on it, to the victor go the spoils. Personally, I think they need to stay focused on what is happening in Iran. I wonder, how do we negotiate when the money run out?

Francismdelvecchio.com

November 10, 2013

President Barack Obama

1600 Pennsylvania Avenue N.W.

Washington D.C. 20500

Dear President Obama,

      The New Your Times printed an article highlighting the rough year you are having and indicated you are a lame duck president. What they did not mention was there are people in this country that have it rougher than you and you are the reason for that. Your difficult days in office are a result of listening to those warped advisors pushing their agenda. I truly doubt if your agenda wants you to look stupid, support flawed and failing programs, and think you can get away with lying to the American people. Even the media can't protect you from looking stupid.

      Senator Graham is going to hold up your appointments until you come clean on Benghazi. I know it doesn't matter to you or Hillary, but the rest of America would like to know the truth. This is another example of putting yourself before the needs of the country. Graham is using the only tactic available to him because you can't man up. What can be worse than getting caught in a lie to the people, getting caught in another lie where four Americans were killed?

      The Obamacare ads do not mention anything about the tax penalty for young people if they don't sign up. They don't mention a repayment of subsidies based on income verification and increases. Do they address what people can do if they lose their insurance and our out of a signup period? Who is responsible for reading and knowing the 2700 pages of the bill and the 27,000 pages of regulations, or is that in the frequent questions asked section of the website?

      You are in India on Veterans Day and you never noted that the Marine Corp was formed 238 years ago. Happy Birthday and Semper Fidelis fellow Marines and to all veterans may this day be a remembrance of all your love and sacrifices for your country. Your, Commander and Chief is in India reciting Muslim prayers with the school children.

Francismdelvecchio.com

November 11, 2013

President Barack Obama

1600 Pennsylvania Avenue N.W.

Washington D.C. 20500

Dear President Obama,

I had a CBS moment when I declared you were in India on Veterans Day. I apologize for the misinformation and my interpretation of the media sources. That said, back to business.

Your environmental advisors have told you that the ethanol program started under Bush and continued by you have caused immeasurable damage to the landscape, the water supply and conservation acreage. The farmers have planted an additional 15 million acres of corn using conservation acreage and global warming have added to the damage. I suggest an intensive investigation into this and you heed the advice of your advisors in this case.

Hassan Rouhani does not call the final shots in Iran, the Ayatollah Ali Khamenei does and he refers to America as the "smiling enemy." Talk is cheap in these negotiations and our allies in Europe and the Middle East, if we have any left, are not supporting the nuclear talks. I suggest you follow the lead of our allies and the senate and push for conclusive indicators. I don't see the upside of dealing with a country that hates us.

Todd Park will testify before congress and his supporters claim the GOP is taking valuable time from him he needs to fix the Health Care website. He is spending valuable time preparing for his testimony. I didn't know you needed coaching to tell the truth and what was he preparing for the last three years. To his credit, he did warn the administration the site wasn't ready.

Marco Rubio is preparing a bill to certify health care navigators to prevent fraud and misinformation to the people. This will require background and credit checks. He wants the insurance industry to help certify their understanding of the law and the limitations on their advice and use of personal information. My question is, what have we been doing for the last three years besides writing 27,000 pages of regulations?

Francismdelvecchio.com

November 12, 2013

President Barack Obama

1600 Pennsylvania Avenue N.W.

Washington D.C. 20500

Dear President Obama,

President Clinton made some common sense remarks about Obamacare and supported the effort by congress to help people keep their current insurance. The Landrieu Bill according to Feinstein is a common sense fix. I haven't heard the words common sense used by congress in a long time. The issue is people have to buy insurance or be fines, taxed is the real word. If I can choose my level of auto insurance, or buy a less expensive phone, why can't I buy a less expensive health care plan? Maybe it is fair, the people the government subsidizes have to buy a certain plan, but my cash should pay for what I want, not what you want. This law was never about insuring people, it was always about CONTROLING PEOPLE.

I believe congress will fix the problem before the people come back and revisit the health care web site. I hope there will be enough time for them to pass a common sense law and let it sit on your desk for 30 days so it can be passed, unless you sign it first. If you don't sign it, will people remember this during the 2014 election or will the democrats still have enough low misinformed democrats to support their reelection? If they do remember and the republicans don't shoot themselves in the foot again, you will have a lot more days to play golf in your last two years.

There will always be an excuse to start a war between Israel and Palestine. They can swap land, stop settlements, and talk all they want, religious differences that fuel the hate between the countries will never be settled. The Israelis should protect what they have and the Palestinians should make the best of what they have. Start teaching the generations to get along and maybe someday they will. Too much hate there.

Kuwait is supporting their favorite war and Al Qaeda. Mteiri, who helped support America in Iraq is helping to rid Syria of Assad. Mteiri chose who he thinks will be the winner. It is all about religion and tribal customs, democracy is just a mask.

Francisdelvecchio.com

November 13, 2013

President Barack Obama

1600 Pennsylvania Avenue N.W.

Washington D.C. 20500

Dear President Obama,

The opium fields in Afghanistan are at record high production, so much for teaching them how to farm other products. The terrorist need the money from these crops to keep their operations going and the Afghan government isn't going to do much about it. Bring the troops home and leave those people to their own devices.

There is a move on to impeach Eric Holder, about time. The man has no regard for the laws of the land and lies like the rest of your administration. He thinks he is above the law like you and many other politicians that have been caught with their hand in the cookie jar. Holder picks and chooses the laws he wants to enforce and gives you lame excuses for his disregard. The man needs to go. The best thing that can happen is they will put his face on the front page and take Obamacare off.

Tell Ms. Sebelius her figures are wrong. You want 7 million people to sign up plus the 5 million who are getting their insurance canceled. The House has a bill and the Senate has a different bill ready to go to protect the people that were canceled, your advisor are going to make an announcement that will supposedly protect these people. If I were you, I would go with the House or Senate plan. Stiller decisions are not coming out of the Whitehouse.

When does the coverage start for the people that sign up after December 15th? I don't see that mentioned anywhere and what will all the people associated with the rollout be doing after March31st? Can you buy insurance on the federal website after March 31st, or will this turn into another multimillion dollar ad campaign?

The Senate, Kerry and you need to get on the same page about Iran. Kerry will look pretty stupid making promises he can't deliver and your clout is gone after Obamacare.

November 14, 2013

President Barack Obama

1600 Pennsylvania Avenue N.W.

Washington D.C. 20500

Dear President Obama,

You created this mess with Obamacare and your administrative fix isn't going to save it from self-destruction. I still question the constitutionality of forcing people to buy something and telling them what they have to buy. You could have kept the conditions in the law, but opened it up to national sales across the country that offered more options for the people. You are trying to control an industry you know nothing about. Your special deals with democrats, back door passage of the law, and lying your way to the rollout has caught up to you and your advisors and you can't stop lying about it.

Your comparison to the Bush handling of Katrina is flawed. Bush tried for three days to convince Governor Blanco to let him send in the 82nd airborne unit to help and she refused every attempt by him. On the sixth day he had to invoke the Insurrection Act to send in federal troops for help. She and you are alike, she needed help and refused it and you need help and continue to put politics over common sense solutions. Stop blaming other people for your shortcomings.

What genius came up with the 93% rule of a target estimate that the government received money from the insurance companies and the 103% rule that the government had to pay the insurance companies? This is supposed to stabilize premiums? Competition creates stability.

Iran is stopping their nuclear program and allowing greater access to the facilities except one, Parchin military site where they are working on triggers for nuclear weapons. Simple, they are either all in or all out. They are buying time and they are not going to throw away billions of dollars in investments away. If they are hurting so bad, where are they getting the money to support terrorist groups? This should be part of the negotiations.

The United Nations is planning to vote on a moratorium on fully autonomous weapons, killer robots, like the x-47B, that doesn't need a pilot to land on an aircraft carrier. They are like you, always telling people how to spend their money.

Francismdelvecchio.com

November 15, 2013

President Barack Obama

1600 Pennsylvania Avenue N.W.

Washington D.C. 20500

Dear President Obama,

The democrats are jumping ship as I predicted they would and the republicans who had a chance to capitalize on new legislation come up with a wimpy bill that lets the insurance companies renew their canceled policies. You had Obama in in your sights and you lets King Obama change the law and make the House and Senate look useless. So why do we need congress if King Obama can do anything he wants. The problem is clearly over his head and the wimpy advisors he depends on. Now the insurance companies need to do a 360 and bail his butt out of trouble. They deserve what they get for supporting the ACA in the first place. It doesn't take a genius to figure out who the big losers will be, the people of course.

The state insurance commissioners have the ball in their court and the blame will follow them. Some states are going to allow the renewals to take place and others will not. The insurance companies are worried about increased premiums in 2015, when did they ever worry about increased premiums? They are worried about reduced profits. This is the Humpty Dumpty syndrome, an administrative fix isn't going to put this mess back together again. DELAY THE ENTIRE BILL FOR ANOTHER YEAR. Nothing good comes out of a quick fix.

Another complication is thousands of doctors have been notified they are not a part of insurance company's coverage. Patients will have to find new doctors and their choices will be limited. This is due to the cuts in Medicare that are supposed to help pay for subsidies. In case you missed this King Obama, those subsidies were already built in to the insurance premiums by the insurance companies.

Karzai is going to present the security agreement the US and he has been working on, that isn't complete, to the Loya Jirga, a group of over 3,000 clergy, tribal leaders and government officials. They will discuss it for several days and decide its fate. I can't imagine what this will be like. Pull the troops out of Afghanistan and leave these 3,000 members to solve their own problems. What is this going to cost making 3,000 people happy?

King Obama, I don't remember reading anywhere in the Constitution where you have the authority to change laws or pick and choose like Eric Holder. This country doesn't need a King, it needs a leader that is not a political pawn.

Francismdelvecchio.com

November 16, 2013

President Barack Obama

1600 Pennsylvania Avenue N.W.

Washington D.C. 20500

Dear President Obama,

The republicans have a great opportunity to fix Obamacare and help you out at the same time. We know you could care less about the people and you have demonstrated that with your continued support of a flawed health care plan. Now the republicans have a chance to right the wrong for the people or will they let you struggle along with the health care plan. Because they are dumb, they will let you and the American people struggle, typical politicians. This is the fix the congress and you should support;

Keep the provisions for preexisting conditions.

Keep the provision which eliminates the cap.

Establish a risk pool for the cap and preexisting conditions and assign it proportionately to the insurance companies.

Allow the insurance companies to sell nationwide with coverage nationwide.

Allow the insurance companies to market minimal and maximal plans that can fit everyone's budget.

Increase the fine and make it mandatory that everyone has health insurance and provide a minimal plan option for the healthy and the young. Everyone pays something.

Subsidize no income and low income individuals and families that will be covered by insurance companies not the government, eliminate Medicaid, the insurance companies and hospital groups will do a better job of providing care and reducing costs.

Establish tort reform to decrease malpractice insurance rates and make it mandatory for excess funds in this insurance pool to adjust future premiums.

Have doctors and nurses set the minimal medical standards for the industry, not insurance companies. This should coincide with the tort reform and malpractice insurance.

These are some of the measures I would institute. The medical industry should abide by minimal standards set by congress and come up with the solutions. They should offer plans that fit people's budget and state of health. You have already passed an important part of the legislation that everyone should have health insurance and the Supreme Court supported this. It is time to let the professionals to come up with the legislation and solutions, not politicians.

Francismdelvecchio.com

November 17, 2013

President Barack Obama

1600 Pennsylvania Avenue N.W.

Washington D.C. 20500

Dear President Obama,

The Volcker Rule, which is supposed to reign in Wall Street, will be completed soon. It has only taken a year to write it. It is supposed to limit risky investments by the banks and shady deals. The rule is simple, no more bail outs for the banks and the banks can't invest depositor's money in high risk and speculative investments. The banks can only invest their massive profits. How do you determine a high risk investment? Put in a grandma clause that states, allowable investment amounts can't exceed the cost of living and care over the person's life expectancy and tie it to the CPI. If grandma has a $100,000.00 and it will cost her $110,000.00 to live out her life, she should be put in a risk free investment that will earn the extra $10,000.00 over the course of her life. If grandma has a million dollars and it will cost her $700,000.00 to live out the rest of her life, only 20% of the $300,000.00 plus excess can be used for risk investments with the persons permission.

Seven million Jews live with approximately nine million Arabs of various backgrounds in Israel. There are 500,000 Jews living with 2.5 million Palestinians in and around the West Bank. There is tension but they all seem to get along. This demonstrates that the people can coexist, but the leadership can't demonstrate the same in their negotiations. Call this what it really is, old leadership arguing over a religious issue when the people have demonstrated their willingness to live together and worship. There will always be hard core factions that war over peace just as there is in America. Are problems are more distant in most cases. If people can live together and respect each other's rights and religion, then let their voice be heard, not a bunch of land negotiators. Tell Kerry to stop dipping in the taxpayer's pocket and adding fuel to the fire.

Mr. President, you are lucky, the republicans are going to make the roll out of Obamacare their battle cry against the democrats. It is as much as their responsibility for this flawed piece of legislation as it is yours. I believe the only people that actually read the bill were the research people for the media and the political foundations. They circled the wagons and took shots at the weakness and controversy of the bill rather than come up with solutions to make it a joint success. This democrat and republican congress is a civil replica of the civil war. Democracy?

www.ingramcontent.com/pod-product-compliance
Lightning Source LLC
Chambersburg PA
CBHW070854290526
45795CB00001B/115